MACRO-MIND POWER

This remarkable book gives you the ancient and one-time secret techniques for releasing the macrocosmic power of your mind.

MACRO-MIND POWER

by

REBECCA CLARK

A. THOMAS AND COMPANY
Wellingborough, Northamptonshire

First published in the United Kingdom 1980
*Original American edition published by
Parker Publishing Company Inc., West Nyack, New York*

ISBN 0 85454 072 5

Printed and bound in Great Britain by
Biddles Ltd., Guildford, Surrey.

Dedication

This book is lovingly and joyously dedicated to the greater expression and fulfillment of life for all people.

May this book light up the Mystic Path to success in every area of your life—money, good health, love, boundless new energy, greater wisdom and understanding, friends, and everything else your heart desires.

You, Dear Reader, at this very moment possess the capacity for miraculous self-enrichment through using the Macrocosmic Power of your mind. *You already have this power;* you only need to exercise it in beneficial ways to enrich your life.

Begin now to use this wonderful Macrocosmic Mind Power and you will experience receiving the abundance of everything good that life has to offer.

How This Book Will Change Your Life

Is there one fantastic Primal Power in the universe whose force can be harnessed and utilized to guide you to ultimate freedom and all the joys of triumphant living?

The answer is an unqualified *Yes!* And it's called *Macro-Mind Power*.

Ancient philosophers always thought of man as a counterpart of the universe and expressed the idea of man's relationship to the universe by the use of two related words—*microcosm* and *macrocosm*. The former meant "little universe" and the latter, "large universe." Upon studying this viewpoint, we can understand the Macrocosm to represent the entire warp and woof of creation. The Macrocosm is the known and the unknown, the visible and the invisible, stretching eternally and encompassing within its framework the entire schema of universes, galaxies, stars, sun systems, planets, and monadic worlds. Perhaps even worlds within worlds.

Of course, next comes the realization that creation by definition implies creator, in the same manner as effect implies cause. Earth man calls the Creator by many names—God, Yahweh, Infinite One, Source, the Cosmic Eye, and so on.

Macrocosmic Mind is the Universal Consciousness that went forth as the Word, the Logos, firing within man, the microcosm, the perfect pattern of man's Divine Identity and establishing the Truth of all the things man can be and do, glorifying the laws of the Universe.

There are two manifestations of Macrocosmic Mind controlling all elements of the Universe.

1. There is the Universal Consciousness, or God Mind, involving certain laws which were established in the beginning of creation and are unwritten, but immutable, laws of the Universe. These laws are fixed in the Universal Consciousness and whenever there is no interference, or no special appli-

cation of the Universal Consciousness, these laws are fulfilled by every element that we find existing in the universe.
2. There is the creative power of man's mind, which is a part of the Universal Creative Power, and this mind power can affect the elements of the Universe by applying other Universal Laws and making the elements obey.

How Macro-Mind Power Can Change Your Life

This remarkable book gives you the ancient and one-time secret techniques for releasing the Macrocosmic Power of your mind.

Know this truth:

> EVERY GOOD THING YOU ARE SEEKING IS ALREADY SEEKING YOU!

You have the power right now to attract all this good into your life. But you must know HOW to use your Macro-Mind Power. You must *learn how to put it into action* to draw to yourself your inmost desires. Here is a step-by-step program of self-help that will thrust you into an affluent and totally new life style.

15 Ways This Book Will Help You

1. James P. turned a fascinating hobby into a million-dollar business. (See Chapter 1.)
2. Dorothy F. used Macro-Mind Magnetism to find a new interest in life and embark on a unique new career. (See Chapter 1.)
3. Vera L. felt a strong precognitive prompting, took immediate action, and saved the life of her three-year-old granddaughter. (See Chapter 2.)
4. Laura T. experienced a vivid dream of a terrible accident. Four days later, during a trip, she recognized the highway upon which she was traveling as the road in her dream, and promptly used Macro-Mind Power to save her life. (See Chapter 5.)
5. Dan K. was under such intense financial strain that he declared bankruptcy. Shortly afterward, he discovered the infinite power of Macrocosmic Mind, overcame his state of

depression, and claimed his abundant good, thereby repaying his creditors. (See Chapter 3.)

6. Nancy L. had been out of work and struggling under deep despondency for several weeks. After realizing that her present state of prosperity was greater than she thought, she began using the powerful prosperity magnetizer of praise and thanksgiving. Not long after, Nancy manifested a fabulous new job which enabled her to pay all her bills in full and vacation in the Virgin Islands! (See Chapter 3.)
7. Jane B. used fantastic prosperity techniques to attract the right buyer for her house, bringing joy to herself and to the purchaser of the house. (See Chapter 4.)
8. Helen H. holds a unique record of having submitted a winning entry in every contest she has entered—including winning prizes of a Hammond organ, trips to New York, Washington, and Europe, and a $50,000 home! (See Chapter 5.)
9. Lewis A. used Macro-Mind Power to overcome and eliminate a racial prejudice and acquire a sincere, life-time friend. (See Chapter 6.)
10. Jim P., vice president of a large manufacturing firm, used Macro-Mind Power to open the door to fantastic financial backing and establishment of his own company with superb salesmen and a top-quality product line. (See Chapter 1.)
11. Sue used Macro-Mind Love Magnetizers to protect her husband from a possible plane crash. (See Chapter 7.)
12. Myrtle F. used the marvelous power of Macrocosmic Mind to heal herself of tuberculosis. (See Chapter 8.)
13. Laura C.'s mother used the awesome power of Macrocosmic Mind to cure an allergic condition of seven years' duration. (See Chapter 9.)
14. Deborah C. blasted the hostility of a jealous woman with the Light of Cosmic Protection and stopped her cold. (See Chapter 10.)
15. Helen C. was attacked by an unknown "evil" force. She began losing weight; her skin turned pallid; and dark circles appeared under her eyes. On a dark night in January she fought for her life with an unseen enemy—and won by dissolving the negative force with Macro-Mind Power "Protection" motivators. (See Chapter 10.)

How Three Vital Elements of Macrocosmic Mind Power Can Benefit You

Three vital elements of Macro-Mind Power are *Desire, Imagination,* and *Faith.* You use these elements many times every day, undoubtedly without realizing that *they have made you what you are,* and *caused you to have what you have* at this point in life. These three faculties will attract everything you need and want when you use them with *deliberate intent.* And that's an important key! *Know your specific desire; see it happening; and believe in Macro-Mind Power to bring it to fruition.*

Start Now to Enjoy a Richer Life

Regardless of what your life is now like, you can start immediately in a new direction:

You can attract an abundance of all good things.

You can enjoy a rich, happy, and successful life.

You can acquire justifiable wealth.

You can adjust or eliminate any problem areas.

You can attract your perfect mate!

You can experience excellent relationships with friends and companions.

You can attract respect and admiration from important people and business associates.

You can set important goals and achieve them!

—and anything else you've ever hoped for!

Macro-Mind Power— The Greatest Power in the Universe

Macrocosmic Mind Power is the greatest power in the universe. It is God-Mind; ever present, all-knowing Mind; the Absolute, and the Unlimited. And all of its manifestations *are the essence of itself.* No other power can compare with it. Whatever you sincerely desire and work for, this wonderful Power can help you achieve. You already have it within you—just waiting to be released and utilized to its fullest manifestation. Put yourself "in gear" with Cosmic

Energy and live a glorious life of success and accomplishment.

Move *in harmony* with Macro-Mind Power and all the good things of life automatically flow into your sphere of existence. It's universal law and it *must work!* Ignore Macro-Mind Power and you face a life frought with frustration and failure. Which way of life do you want? *The choice is up to you!*

How to Solve Your Problems

Every problem has a solution. Every situation has an answer. I definitely believe the information presented in this book will help *you* find the guidance you are seeking. You want to live a more rewarding life. *You can!*

Read how a young businesswoman increased her monthly salary 200% within a short period of time. Read how a novelist gets marvelous ideas through working with Macro-Mind Magnetizers. Read how prayer changed the life of a man standing at death's door. And you'll find many other examples of the successful use of Macro-Mind Power.

Lifetime Guidance You'll Find in This Book

FACTS	A presentation of Cosmic Truths which are unchanging Universal Laws, omnipresent and active in your life.
TECHNIQUES & EXERCISES	These are Divine Blueprints setting forth fully defined plans for the opulent rooms in your mansion of perfect living and riches. They are mighty instructions for using your Macro-Mind Power.
PERSONAL X-RAYS	Self-analysis thoughts and questions are aimed at helping you discover your *Real Self* and stimulate your immediate growth and prosperity.
QUESTIONS & ANSWERS	Recurring questions I've

	been asked by many clients and persons attending lectures and classes are likely to reflect questions which occur to you. A clear, concise answer follows each question.
TRUE CASE HISTORIES	Real life experiences which show how the seemingly magical power of Macrocosmic Mind effectively worked for others and *can work for you.*
CHECKLISTS	Special development tools to help you speedily scan key data regarding your immediate plans, goals, desires, potentials, and ideals.
MACRO-MIND MOTIVATORS	A quick review at the end of each chapter of primal ideas and affirmations presented. They are marvelous reminders and can be used for a quick brush-up occasionally.

This book can change your life! It is written to help you. It offers keys to Health, Wealth, Happiness, and Success. *Will you use them?*

Thirteen chapters offer atom-smashing ideas presented in simple, practical, down-to-earth language. Easy techniques and exercises are presented for employing Macro-Mind Power to bring forth a feeling of complete inner satisfaction and fulfillment and manifestation of all the good you desire.

This book is a workbook for you. The more you personalize it, the more it will help you. First you read and learn; then you *practice* what you have learned. Apply the Macro-Mind Motivators lavishly and embark on a great and wonderful adventure in mental and spiritual unfoldment. Take a rich journey into a new world—a world of Success!

God bless you tremendously and permanently!

Rebecca Clark

Contents

1

The Cosmic Secret of Macrocosmic Mind Power

The Greatest Secret on Earth!

What is the greatest secret on earth, and how can you use its powerful magic formula effectively in your life?

The greatest secret on earth is *The Miracle of Macrocosmic Mind Power*. Unlocking its magic formula unleashes its fantastic effectiveness in your life and affairs when you *contact* this Universal Power, *learn* the amazing laws dictated by It, *understand* the principles of Its use, and *apply* the unfailing wisdom of what you learn in your world every single day!

Think for a moment about how the average person spends the hours of his day. Scientists have likened his actions to that of a pendulum—swinging back and forth and not making much progress. Favorable events occur in his life; perhaps someone pays him a meaningful compliment, he receives an unexpected gift, he is surprised by a slight increase in salary, and our man feels good. Then, perhaps, some situation occurs which alters his thinking and the next moment, the compliment seems insincere, the unexpected gift is one that isn't really that useful, and the slight increase in salary falls far short of providing enough financial substance to meet the increasing demands of his world. Under the heavy weight of this kind of thinking, the average person allows his feelings to swing like the pendulum and become feelings of sadness, depression, or perhaps of unworthiness. And his day vacillates from an "up" and happy frame of mind to a "down" and depressed mental state. The average man fluctuates between confidence and uncertainty, between decision and indecision, between cheerfulness and gloom, between peaceful calmness and frustration.

Often these feelings are followed by further feelings of futility, hopelessness, or being trapped on a vicious merry-go-round of existence. And that isn't living!

But you are free to live! You never have to accept the pathetic pendulum swing. You never have to accept seeming limitation in any manner!

You are free to be, to do, to accept, to reject. You are free to be the prosperous, effective, kind, loving, exciting, successful person you want to be. You are free to take actions which you consider wise and will in no way harm or hinder another person. You are free to do the things which will lead you into paths of poise, peace, serenity, and satisfaction. You are free to do your part in bringing joy, happiness, creativeness, and expression into the world!

You are free to decide for something, or to decide against it. Nothing can bind you, nothing can restrict you, unless you allow it to. No person, place, or situation can limit you or your good—unless you accept the limitation! And what is true for you is also true for every other living soul on this planet earth. Even as you are free, others, too, are free.

A housewife told me one day how she conditioned her mind with the following affirmation and reestablished her sense of freedom from routine and unglamorous duties.

> **The peace of Macrocosmic Mind fills my own mind and heart, and I meet the demands of everyday life calmly, confidently, and happily. I am a free soul and I claim my freedom.**

You mentally and verbally influence everything in your world. This smart lady was using the power of the spoken word combined with a powerful positive attitude to create contentment in her life.

Macro-Mind Power—Your Link with Eternity

With the passing of time comes a reminder of the setting in which human lives are placed, and the thinking person becomes aware of his relationship with eternity. Your life may appear to be governed by events and circumstances that surround you, but your true port of anchorage is not in things temporal, but in things eternal. To stand firm in this belief, to hold to the Truth of the

Universe—especially in today's world—is often difficult and really tests your faith. But it can be done!

Life is permanent. It does not change. Yet, manifestations of life do change because they are impermanent. When you reach the point of regaining consciousness of your true Macrocosmic identity, you will know that manifestation changes with the changes that take place within your mind.

> YOU ARE GOING TO LEARN HOW TO ALIGN YOUR MIND WITH MACROCOSMIC MIND AND THE REALITY OF THE UNIVERSE AND NEVER AGAIN BE MISLED BY THINGS THAT ARE UNREAL!

The metaphysical truth is that all life is one. A true Macrocosmic indivisible whole. All is Mind—one Universal Mind. And all is *now*—the eternal now.

The matchless Creator of all there is has designed your life on the scale of eternity rather than on the scale our earth time shows. Your increasing awareness of mankind's link between time and eternity can provide a powerful stimulus to all kinds of love, happiness, and abundance in your life right now. Your increasing awareness can provide the impetus needed to go forth to improve your life and the lives of others with whom you come in daily contact!

You are Macrocosmic Mind in infantile environment, currently wrapped in swaddling garments. Time is a swaddling garment. Space is a swaddling garment. Flesh is a swaddling garment. So, too, are the outer senses and the things perceivable through these channels. A benevolent mother or father can look at their baby wrapped in swaddling garments and know with certainty that the swaddling garments are not the baby, nor even a part of the baby. However, they are present for a purpose—the purpose of aiding growth. But the baby doesn't realize this fact. The baby only feels the restrictions of the swaddling garments and vigorously rebels against the restrictions.

Thoughts are things, and they are just as important as actions. And erroneous thinking is just as powerful as correct thinking. The way you think makes you what you are and thereby profoundly influences the world around you!

A famous general was greatly concerned about the outcome of an important battle, so he decided he would question a giant computer about the event. He carefully pushed all the proper controls and boldly asked the question, "Will we win or lose?"

Lights blinked, buzzers buzzed, and the computer paused, then spit forth the answer, "Yes!"

Eagerly the general reached for the replay, read it, then read it again, and after a moment roared in exasperation, "Yes, WHAT?"

Again the computer flashed and blinked its lights, buzzed its buzzers, paused, then barked right back, "Yes, SIR!"

This may seem ridiculous, but have you asked yourself the same question, "Will I win or will I lose?" and life barks back the answer, "Yes, SIR!"

You see, the average person expects that life will be made up of a few wins here and a few losses there, all the while fervently hoping he can win a few more times than he loses.

When you understand the Universal Law of Cause and Effect—WHAT YOU GIVE FORTH, SO YOU GET BACK—you cease receiving double talk from your computer. You receive positive, workable, affirmative truth you can use in your life.

We each have a memory factor deep within the subjective area of our mind. Like the computer, it adds up all the winning thoughts and all the losing thoughts that have been deposited in it since your life began, and then delivers you the verdict of your own belief.

YOUR MIND IS YOUR LINK WITH ETERNITY. Time is the golden thread of life experiences on which you string the colorful beads of events. Time has been compared to a Janus with one face looking forward and the other face looking backward. The forward look depicts future time and the backward look depicts past time. If you gaze too intently into the future, you may unearth apprehensions—you may grow old and unattractive to the opposite sex, you may not be as effective and efficient as you are now, you may not achieve the material aspects of life you desire. And like a beautiful bird charmed by a snake, most people flutter and protest before the seeming venom of time, little realizing that they can lift their wings and fly free!

True time is eternal. There are no restrictions! There are no limitations! You are ever living in the *now.* Ten seconds ago is past time, ten seconds ahead is future time. And you can't get there from here! You can only live right now!

You are presently the accumulation of all your life experiences. You are the same identity as when you entered this world through birth in this span of time, and you shall still be the same identity upon transition. Your identity as a unique individual is never taken away. The goal is to expand your awareness and make your life expressive and meaningful.

Becoming aware of the truth about eternity and your place in its vastness frees and releases you from restrictions. When you use the power of Macrocosmic Mind, your faculties expand, your soul rejoices, and your body thrills to the realization that there can be no defeat, no end. Your progress as a human being is as eternal as life, and life and growth are one.

Why You Should Know You Are Divine!

Doesn't it make sense that if you really *know* something, you walk forward with greater confidence, greater assurance, and increased capacity to accomplish your desires!

You are a child of the *living* God—the omnipotent, Macrocosmic Creator of everything there is. You are born of God. You are Divine. You have all power, all ability, all capacity to do God-like things. Psalms 82:6 says,

> I have said, Ye are Gods; and all of you are children of the Most High.

Think about this. Can you imagine anything greater, more powerful than realizing your true heritage, and then stepping forward to claim it! It is vastly important for you to *know* that the fountainhead from which we draw *all* our good is Macrocosmic Mind. It is the Omnipotent, Omnipresent, and Omniscient Source.

Question: What does it mean to be an heir of God? And to what are we heirs?

Answer: To be an heir of God means we, as His children, share abundantly, equally in the complete estate of our Father-Creator. *We are heirs to all the substance in the Universe. And substance is the stuff things are produced from!*

Yet, it is up to you to claim your inheritance, for in order to realize the manifestation of your inheritance you must first lay claim to it. This is accomplished through *Desire*, *Imagination*, and *Faith*. Here is your universal formula for success:

Desire, Imagination, and Faith equals Successful Achievement

Remember it and *Use* it often! If you do, everything you need and shall ever need, everything you desire and shall ever desire, is right within your reach through the realm of your thoughts and the miracle-working power of Macrocosmic Mind.

DIVINE MIND ALWAYS HAS,
DIVINE MIND ALWAYS WILL,
SUPPLY YOUR EVERY NEED.

You may desire things that do not seem to be within your reach for you may see them as belonging to someone else, or they may seem to be beyond your present capacity for attainment at a particular stage of development.

BUT ANYTHING RIGHTEOUSLY DESIRED MUST ULTIMATELY COME WITHIN YOUR REACH AS YOU APPLY YOUR ENERGIES IN RIGHT THINKING, RIGHT FEELING, RIGHT WORDS, AND RIGHT ACTIONS TOWARD ITS ATTAINMENT.

You never have to desire that which belongs to someone else, you never have to "take away" anything from another person. Every good thing you desire is available for you from your own source of supply. Your job is to prepare your consciousness for the acceptance of the things you desire by seeking to understand the underlying universal laws back of your achieving what you wish.

When I arrived in Lynchburg to establish a new ministry in an area where no ministry had been before, my nucleus from which to build a full-fledged growing church was a group of about twenty of the most interested, enthusiastic, eager people I've ever met, and the *mountain-moving power of Macrocosmic Mind.* We began holding our services in a rented meeting room of a local motel. Within two months, our congregation had multiplied several times in number, we were meeting all our expenses (and one beautiful soul gave a lovely, large love offering for the purpose of establishing a savings account), and a real estate agent called requesting the opportunity to show me a church building which had just come on the market for sale! Things happened rapidly. I looked at the building; it was absolutely perfect for our needs but we couldn't afford to purchase it at that time. Immediately I began working with the power of Macrocosmic Mind through prosperity and divine order affirmations.

An appointment was scheduled with the owners of the church building. Our needs and desires were explained. The owners of the building held a brief meeting and the results were that they would agree to lease the building to us for six months with the option to purchase it at the end of that time. All monies paid for rent during this six-month period would apply toward the purchase price of the building.

In two months we had demonstrated growth in numbers, fantastic financial support, and our very own church building!

The whole idea and manifestation simply boils down to this:

> YOU MUST HAVE AN INNER REALIZATION THAT MACROCOSMIC MIND (GOD) AS SUBSTANCE IS YOUR INEXHAUSTIBLE SOURCE OF SUPPLY AND YOU CAN CALL THE FULFILLMENT OF YOUR NEEDS INTO MANIFESTATION.

Use the following affirmation:

> **God is in charge of my life and affairs. I fully trust Macrocosmic Mind to fulfill all my needs. I am quickened, inspired, and uplifted.**

How to Discover and Use Your Macro-Mind Power

From observing case histories over the years and intensively studying in many areas, I now *KNOW that every individual does have the ability to influence the events that shape his future,* and this ability is called *The Law of Mind Action.*

Question: What is it, and how does it work?

If you desire to understand the Law of Mind Action, you must first understand the manifestations of Macrocosmic Mind. I want to reiterate some important facts which were presented in the introduction of this book.

1. Macrocosmic Mind—The Universal Principle which includes all other principles, is the first phase of the law of Mind Action. There is in Reality only one Mind, sometimes called Spirit, which is life, intelligence, power, and creativity in the entire Universe. Yet, the second phase of the Law of Mind Action includes a very important manifestation in

which we are individual, and yet remain a part of the whole. We are free wills and not puppets and can exercise the use of our free will.

2. Mind—meaning man—is that fantastic tool which operates through your brain. Here is the starting point of your every act, spoken word, thought, or feeling.

Charles Fillmore, co-founder of the Unity Movement, describes mind in the following manner:

> The mind is the seat of perception of the things we see, hear, and feel. It is through the mind that we see the beauties of the earth and sky, or music, of art, in fact, of everything. That silent shuttle of thought working in and out through cell and nerve weaves into one harmonious whole the myriad moods of mind, and we call it life.

What a beautiful definition of mind! What a marvelous understanding of these two manifestations of the Universal Mind, controlling all the elements of the Universe. First, there is the Universal Consciousness, or Macro-Mind, with certain immutable laws which were established in the beginning of creation and are unwritten, but ever-present, laws of the Universe. These laws are fixed in the Universal Consciousness and whenever there is no interference, or no special application of the Universal Consciousness, these laws are fulfilled by every element that we find existing in the universe. Second, there is the creative power of man's mind, which is a part of the Universal Creative Power, and this mind power can affect the elements of the Universe by applying other existing Universal Laws and compelling the elements to obey.

How does it work? Let's say that the involved elements are like a large bowling ball. Imagine you are in a bowling alley with a long, smooth bowling lane ahead of you. If you stand at one end of the bowling lane and roll the ball along the floor swiftly and smoothly, it will roll in a straight line to the opposite end of the lane. In taking this action, the ball is following a Universal Law of Cause and Effect.

For example: You roll the ball down the bowling lane and the directive force you use propels it in a straight line toward the opposite end of the lane. Now, if you place an obstacle like a brick on the floor in the middle of the lane and try to roll the ball in a straight line, when the ball strikes the brick, it will be pushed aside and veer from the straight line of previous travel. Thus, the brick is an interference in the way of the ball and in the fulfillment of the natural laws. In putting the brick on the bowling lane, *you used your own mind to direct the Universal Law, or in other words, to modify its operation!*

This same analogy holds true in your thinking. You, as the "roller" of the ball, shepherd your thoughts and ascertain that they are positive and good, or you allow erroneous thinking to cause you to veer from the direct path of accomplishment and fulfillment.

Question: How does the Law of Mind Action affect man and his universe?

Answer: Thinking is the connecting link between Macrocosmic Mind and man.

It makes a great deal of difference in your daily life what you think about God, about yourself, about your neighbors, about your work associates, in fact, about everything. One expression of Macrocosmic Mind is through the golden glimmer of divine ideas. Therefore,

THINKING IS THE MOVEMENT OF IDEAS WITHIN YOUR MIND, OR YOUR INTELLECT IN ACTION.

From these ideas you form mental images or pictures in your mind, based on your acquired understanding, which are then brought forth as *desires and actions.*

Your thinking is a creative force which is constantly at work in man and in all creation. Mental atmosphere is produced by the kind of thoughts you use, and it draws to itself thoughts and ideas that are like its own nature. *This magnetic atmosphere of thought travels with you and is a part of you!* Power from your thoughts flows forth to touch others and has its effect for either beneficial or derogatory purposes—depending upon your own interest and intent, and the receptivity of the one receiving the thought energy.

Your Thoughts Are the Molders of Your World!

Every experienced metaphysician knows that man's mind molds from an omnipresent element everything which takes form, shape, and intelligence and becomes a part of his thought world. The knowledge and awareness that your world is composed of what you have idealized should make you more watchful of the activities of your mind, thereby laying the groundwork for a bigger, better, more productive, more affluent life!

> Do not be conformed to this world but be transformed by the renewal of your mind, that you may prove what is the will of God, what is good and acceptable and perfect.
>
> Romans 12:2 (RSV)

Recently, I talked with Dorothy F., a young woman of twenty-five who, three years ago, seemingly had a dozen strikes against her. Dorothy had lost her husband through a tragic automobile accident and was left with two small children to support. She had very little money, no job, a high school education, no formal training, and very few years of plain old life experience.

Dorothy came to counsel with me shortly after her husband's death and seemed to be at a rock-bottom level of depression. As we talked, she described her feelings and desire to work with people somehow in a close, fulfilling manner, but she had no idea of how to go about making her dream a reality.

Shortly after we began working together, an opportunity came for Dorothy to visit an old friend who was living in Pennsylvania. The invitation also included an offer for Dorothy to work in an historic old hotel for three months during the summer. Dorothy had a good feeling about the invitation, and so did I. Care for the children would be no problem since they had been invited to visit their paternal grandparents in the country during the summer.

Dorothy had managed to save a small amount of money—enough to cover her expenses for the time she would be gone—so, she decided to invest this small savings as "seed money" toward her future. She delivered the children to their grandparents, allowed a friend who was looking for a place to live the use of her home, and happily left for Pennsylvania.

Upon arriving at her destination, Dorothy was given a pleasant room and the position of desk clerk in the hotel. While performing her duties as desk clerk, she had the opportunity to meet all the guests of the hotel. One guest was a handsome young man who was a junior executive with J. C. Penney Company. He was impressed by the genuineness of Dorothy's smile and friendly attitude. Since he needed a secretary, he offered her a position with his firm beginning shortly after the close of the hotel at the end of summer. Dorothy accepted the offer, returned to Virginia to pick up her children, and moved to New Jersey. About a year later, she married the man and they have a lovely life!

Often it is necessary to dare to be different, to dare to step out on faith, to dare to follow the inner promptings which are trying to give you guidance if you will listen.

Dorothy's miracle-working affirmation was:

> **I have confidence in my God-given guidance. All Good is for me, and I claim my good now! Infinite wisdom guides, blesses, and prospers me, and I am successful in all activities I undertake!**

It worked! And I say, show me a man or a woman with a powerful all-consuming dream, and link this with a deep, unshakable faith in MACRO-MIND POWER, and I'll show you a champion mountain-mover!

The Law of Macro-Mind Magnetism

Did you know that you posses thousands of times more Magnetic Power than does the most powerful magnet ever made by man? And did you also know that *your use* of the magnetic power of your own mind has caused you to become what you are, where you are, how you are, and why you have the things you have! A definite hard statement of fact? You're darn right—and every word is true!

Within the past decade, scientists who explore into the vast reaches of the mind have discovered that the magnetic power within man can be controlled and directed toward changing man into a fantastic new person.

> YOUR MACRO-MIND POWER MAKES IT POSSIBLE FOR YOU TO ATTRACT TO YOURSELF ANY AND ALL OF LIFE'S ABUNDANCE.

But you must learn how to control this Macro-Mind Power, this dynamic mental magnetism. You must learn how to direct its power toward constructive, meaningful, and desirable goals and through the power of your own actions, cause a miraculous change for the better to take place in your life.

Every manifestation begins in your mind! I can't say that too often. Start now to school your impulses and feelings into desired areas. Your dreams and ideals are the parents of your impulses and your feelings. What you think concerning people, places, situations, and things takes shape in your life. Never entertain a thought for someone else which you would not have objectified in yourself. YOU ARE THE ASSEMBLAGE OF YOUR THOUGHTS!

The thoughts of your conscious mind are definite instructions presented to the subconscious mind, which carries them out by projecting them onto the screen of your life!

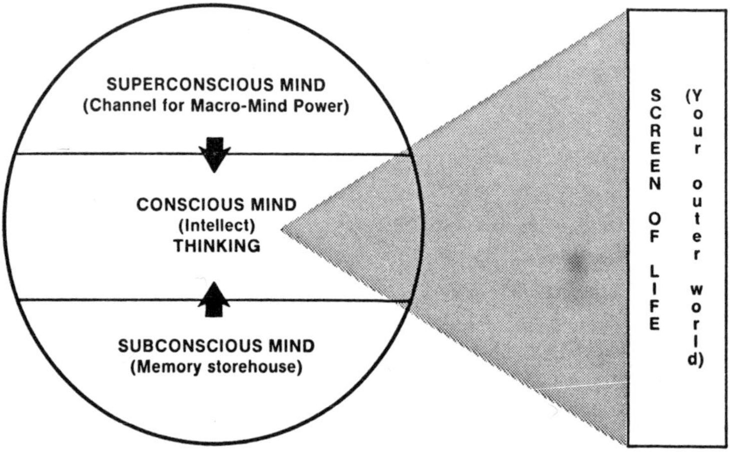

Let's look at the three aspects of your mind and see how they work.

A. SUPERCONSCIOUS—The mind that knows all and is able to accomplish all things because it is one with Macrocosmic Mind. Here resides the pure, unconditioned life energy substance—the same creative material from which thoughts are manifested into things. *Here is your field of great inspiration!* Superconscious Mind supplies you with divine ideas—ideas that have all the makings for perfect and beautiful manifestations in your life.

B. CONSCIOUS—This is the place where you are actively

aware of your thoughts. This aspect of your mind lets you know of all your mental operations and states of consciousness. *Here you establish your identity.* Conscious Mind plays tag between Superconscious and Subconscious Mind. *If you want to control your life, take command of Conscious Mind and consciously, and emphatically determine to think in accord with Superconscious!*

C. SUBCONSCIOUS—Here resides your memory body. The Subconscious aspect of your mind is the home of your feeling nature, your emotions. It is the vast storehouse of all past thoughts and experiences. Your Subconscious Mind perpetrates the body functions such as circulation, breathing, digestion, and so on. You may not always be conscious of everything that takes place in your Subconscious Mind, but Macrocosmic Mind can work perfectly in it unless you gum up the works with ignorant thinking! *Therefore, your Subconscious Mind receives the mental impressions you consciously impress upon it and returns them to you as conscious personal experiences!*

How Macro-Mind Power Can Change Your Life!

Some so-called "lucky" people seem to flow along the road of life constantly progressing to greater successes, riches, rewards, happiness, and fulfillment of their desires. These people demonstrate a fantastic ability to *accomplish their goals* because, knowingly or unknowingly, they are tapping into the dynamic stream of irresistible universal energy. YOU CAN TAP INTO THIS SAME STREAM OF ENERGY! It's right there, flowing all though your life, just waiting to be used. YOU HAVE ONLY TO RECOGNIZE ITS PRESENCE, REALIZE ITS TREMENDOUS VALUE, REACH OUT, AND USE IT! Remember the Macro-Mind success formula:

Desire, Imagination, and Faith equals Successful Achievement.

When you take the action of using this success formula, the fulfillment of your hopes and dreams is not a matter of chance, but a matter of decided application whereby *you gain control over the events in your life.*

Jim P. was a businessman who definitely believed that it was absolutely right to be prosperous. In fact, he felt everybody should have an abundance of good in life. One of his favorite quotes was from Russell H. Conwell's famous lecture, "Acres of Diamonds."

> I say you ought to be rich; you have no right to be poor. To live and not be rich is a misfortune and it is doubly a misfortune because you could have been rich just as well as being poor. . . . We ought to get rich if we can by honorable methods, and these are the only methods that sweep us quickly toward the goal of riches.

One Monday morning, Jim and I were sitting in his lavish executive office (he was vice president of his firm) talking about the tremendous power and effectiveness of Macrocosmic Mind. A telephone call interrupted our conversation and when the call was completed, Jim dropped the receiver onto its cradle and heaved a heavy sigh. An irate customer had been on the other end of the line. Shaking his head in frustration, Jim stared at me and remarked, "I feel so damn helpless sometimes! Here is a customer who placed a hundred-thousand dollar order with our firm three months ago and I can't seem to persuade the shipping department to get the merchandise enroute to the man's store!"

A pregnant silence ensued for about two minutes as we each became enmeshed in our individual thoughts. As Jim raised his eyes and looked at me, I threw the question to him, "Why don't you start your own business?"

The bomb dropped! Inasmuch as I had known Jim and his family for eight years, and had listened to many recitations of his dream of "someday" owning his own furniture manufacturing business, I felt O.K. in making such a statement. Jim had the "know-how" and remarkable ability to accomplish his dream, but he was the world's greatest procrastinator! We talked for several hours that day. Before leaving his office, I gave him the following Macro-Mind affirmation with which to work.

> **I am now open and receptive to the rich, divine ideas flowing to me from Macrocosmic Mind. I am wonderfully equipped to bring these divine ideas into manifestation with ease and assurance. Nothing can defeat me. I give thanks right now for perfect, immediate success. I pronounce this business ven-**

ture and everything connected with it good. Thank you, Father.

About six months later, I received a telephone call from Jim. He was bubbling with excitement. He had decided to put the Macro-Mind success formula to work and use the affirmation I had given him. His desire was strong, his imagination vivid, and he stepped forward with marvelous faith. He had resigned his position as vice president and was starting his own company!

A year passed. One day, I received an impressive-looking envelope in my mail. Opening it with building excitement, I read an invitation to attend the opening ceremonies for Jim's new business showroom in the largest merchandise mart of the furniture industry! The accompanying note told me Jim had acquired secure financial backing, an assemblage of top sales representatives, an efficient manufacturing plant, and a line of quality products. Fantastically, Jim was on his way to becoming a millionaire with *his very own company!*

His note ended with these remarks: "I do hope you will come and see what using the micracle-working power of Macrocosmic Mind has done for me. Each day I tuned in as you suggested. Each day I used the affirmation. Everything I have needed—and more—has been miraculously provided. There was a lot of work to do and never could I have accomplished this alone. Now I know that with God as my teammate, and Macrocosmic Power as my tool, there is no limit to the realization of my dreams! Bless you for your help!"

The Law of Opportunity

Science is constantly unveiling more and more of the mysteries of creation. Each discovery lures mankind on to ever deeper and ever expanding searching. The penetration of each mystery opens for man more profound situations which challenge his intellectual capacity. As he follows the path of investigation, like a pilgrim climbing a rugged mountain, new vistas of knowledge unfold. As each mountain peak is crested, another peak, loftier still, appears on the horizon.

OPPORTUNITIES ARE EVERYWHERE, AND OPPORTUNITIES CARRY NO LIMITATIONS!

The secret to the fulfillment of your every need lies in your responsiveness to the nudgings of the power of Macrocosmic Mind within you. *You are imbued with divine power to achieve any goal you desire.*

The past is gone. Release it and let it be. This is a time for beginning, a time for starting anew. Withdraw your attention from outer appearances and conditions and direct your attention to the power within. This may seem somewhat difficult at first, for you may be accustomed to focusing your attention on your surroundings and the physical aspects of life, and may not have realized that opportunity is knocking at your door. In fact, Opportunity knocks so hard sometimes, it darn near breaks the door down!

Move into the *active* phase of living. Say "YES!" to life! Say "YES!" to all the good things you desire. Say "YES!" to opportunity, and say it with emphasis and enthusiasm and strong determination that you're gonna get it!

Helen Keller refused to accept any kind of limitation in her life. Although she was deprived of her senses of sight and hearing as an infant, she became aware of the vast reservoir of her fertile mind. She began to use the rich substance of this marvelous mind, and her blue eyes could probably "see" a hundred times more clearly than most people can see; and her deaf ears could "hear" the glorious flowing crescendos and full harmonies of orchestral music! With powerful clarity the notes of the lyric soprano touched her inner hearing and she was able to grasp the humor of a stage play.

Helen Keller lived a meaningful life and accomplished immeasurable good throughout the world. Through prayer and meditation, she awakened the inner eye of her soul and uplifted the hearts and minds of the deaf and blind everywhere. She contributed joy, faith, and hope to thousands of people. Many persons who have full use of their eyes and ears have not accomplished a portion as much. She refused to feel unfortunate, or discriminated against. Helen Keller felt there was no such thing as underprivileged or overprivileged. Her feeling was that all were children of the universe and the universe plays fair! She said:

> Dark as my path may seem to others, I carry a magic light in my heart. Faith, the spiritual strong searchlight, illumines the

way. Although sinister doubts lurk in the shadow, I walk unafraid toward the Enchanted Wood where the foilage is always green; where joy abides; where nightingales nest and sing, and where life and death are one in the presence of the Lord.

How to Believe in Your Power of Attraction

It is a scientifically proven fact that if you don't have faith and belief in yourself, it's certain no one else will! I spoke these words one day to a prominent senator when I worked for the state government. His booming reply almost knocked me off my feet!

"You're darn sure right! I've never had any problem in realizing that truth in my whole life!"

And it was true. He was a dynamo of energy, vitality, and accomplishment.

Question: Why is it vital that you believe in yourself?

Answer: Because if you don't believe in yourself, it will be impossible for you to believe in the miracle-working power of your mind, and in the tremendous good it can do for you and the unlimited success it can bring you.

To strengthen faith in yourself, I am going to ask you to write the following affirmation on a three by five white card and carry it in your pocket or purse. Several times during the day, pull out the card, read the words quietly to yourself, concentrate for a moment on the truth of the words, then release the thought and go about your affairs of the day.

I believe in myself. I have faith that I can accomplish whatever I make up my mind to do. Starting right now, I affirm that I can use Macro-Mind Power to attract all things that will benefit me and my personal good. All that is mine by divine right now flows to me in rich abundance. There is no delay! I am open and receptive and ready to receive my good!

You already have the seed of faith within you as a power center. It is a divine gift from God and knows only complete assurance. Faith is dauntless and cannot know defeat! It has the insight to pierce through the confusion of that which is visible to *Know* the strength and certainty of the invisible.

THE FOUNDATION FOR FAITH IN YOURSELF IS THE TRUTH THAT YOU ARE A MAGNIFICENT CHILD OF GOD AND, AS SUCH, INHERIT THE DIVINE NATURE AND THE DYNAMIC POWER OF MACROCOSMIC MIND.

Realizing the Divine Promise

A story is told of a prince who was kidnapped at birth from his father's palace. Raised in poverty in a wretched village, the young prince soon rebelled against the poverty in his life. As he grew into young manhood, he carefully constructed a plan for becoming king of the land. He became an adult and through a series of schemes and bloody battles, he finally won the throne. But he wasn't happy. He was anxious, hostile, and fearful that some other ambitious person could come along and take his throne from him as he had taken it from another. He lived in dread, and his life was day-to-day misery.

One day an old begger arrived at the palace kitchen and told a strange story of a kidnapped prince and alluded to the fact that the kidnapped prince was none other than the present monarch! The beggar was brought before the king and the king learned his true identity and that he was in reality a king by birthright. Immediately he realized the folly of trying to retain by force that which he possessed as a natural inheritance. With his newly gained insight he began to change and developed a truly kingly consciousness. He had no fear, no feeling of being threatened, only quiet dominion.

You are a king or a queen. You are a child of royal birth. You are an off-spring of Macrocosmic Mind. Until this truth becomes a realization in your own consciousness, you will not know yourself enough to trust yourself, to have faith in your abilities, to be assured of eternal safety, prosperity, peace, and well-being. *The error in your mind which causes you to assume you are anything less than the child of a king is the source of every misunderstanding in life that perplexes you!*

Aldoux Huxley once remarked,

> It is because we don't know who we are, because we are unaware that the Kingdom of Heaven is within us, that we behave in the generally silly, the often insane, the sometimes

> criminal ways that are so characteristically human. We are saved, we are liberated and enlightened, by perceiving the hitherto unperceived good that is already within us, by returning to our eternal Ground and remaining where, without knowing it, we always have been.

What would your life be like if you had no fear? Start this very moment to think and feel and act as if fear dared not exist in your life! What would your life be like if you had all the abundance you desired and needed? Start right now to think and feel and act like the world's greatest millionaire! What would your life be like if you knew with an absolute certainty that no one could ever harm you in any manner? Start right now to think and feel and act as though you are encompassed in a gigantic bubble of the divine light of protection! How would you think and feel and act toward yourself if you knew, without a doubt, that you were a magnificent person, entitled to all the good the universe has in store for you? Start right now to think and feel and act in this manner! How would you react to so-called misfortunes or hurtful experiences if you could see their total inability to interfere in your progress? Take hold of your life right now and think and feel and act in this manner!

These are kingly states of consciousness. As you begin to live with them in your life, you begin to think, to feel, to act, and to look like a king or a queen.

> NOW IS THE TIME TO DO SOMETHING ABOUT YOUR DREAMS, YOUR HOPES, YOUR DESIRES. NOW IS THE TIME TO DO SOMETHING ABOUT YOUR INHERITANCE AS A CHILD OF THE UNIVERSE AND OF GOD. NOW IS THE TIME TO BREAK THROUGH INTO THE KIND OF LIFE YOU DESIRE!

And I believe there isn't a person alive who wouldn't like to have a better life in some way. *Wouldn't you?* Why should you accept the mundane in life when you can experience the total esctasy of magnificent living!

The miracle of Macrocosmic Mind is the true resurrecting power and life flowing through you right here and right now. You can use this power Now! You can prove its effectiveness in your life Now! You don't have to wait a day, a week, a month, or a year. *Now is the time.* You have so much to learn, so much to discover, so much to do, that like the endless ocean, life beckons you constantly to new horizons. Take the time to look at where you are. Everyday people, places, and things are inspiring experiences and signposts to greater growth.

Remember and use the Macro-Mind success formula:

> **Desire, Imagination, and Faith equals Successful Achievement.**

How Your Life Can Become An Exciting Adventure!

Accept the truth that there is a better way to live! Every man, woman, and child, *without exception,* senses that there is more to life than what seems to be currently manifesting. The greatest evidence that there is more is mankind's constant search for the illusive "more." *And when you seek, you find.* This is a universal principle of truth. *The call compels the answer!*

O.K., what is the requirement for you to possess the greatest secret on earth? It isn't a huge bank account (that comes later!), nor youth, nor great strength—none of these things. It is simply your sincere desire and willingness to learn something new; to be open and receptive to truth ideas as they are presented to you; and then to be equally willing to test them *in your own life.*

It works! This isn't merely my personal opinion. I've taught, counseled, lived, and worked with many persons who have proven the powerful working of Macrocosmic Mind in their own life. Therefore, your life transformation will be in exact proportion to the amount of truth you absorb and use without running away!

Five Easy Steps for Developing Macro-Mind Magnetism

1. FAITH—Begin right now to believe with even greater intensity than ever before that all the good you are seeking is also seeking you. Faith is simply the perceiving power of the mind linking with Macro-Mind power to shape manifested substance from invisible substance. Faith is the magnetic power that draws your heart's desire to you from the universe.

2. DESIRE—Decide what it is that you want to have or wish to accomplish. Make this desire the most important thing you've ever desired and know it is yours right now. Make up your mind that you *can* and *will* attract it to you.
3. IMAGINATION—Now imagine a large white screen in your mind and project a mental image of your desire on this screen. Make your projection vivid in living color and as detailed as possible. Your projected desire could be a lovelier home, a better job, more money, nice clothes, good health, a happy marriage, increased understanding, exciting friendships—whatever you feel is your most cherished desire. Form a mental picture of your desire in your conscious mind and project it on your magic screen. Be specific about what you want and put in all the details.
4. FEELING—Now, as you look at your pictured desire on your magic mind screen, inject this desire with a powerful dose of *feeling*. Let all the feelings you expect to experience upon attainment of your desire flow forth. Feel the joy it will bring you. Feel the meaning your desire will bring into your life and this action on your part will give life essence and power to your desire. The magnetic attraction between you and what you desire becomes an activity of the Universal Law of Cause and Effect. You are setting up the cause with your mind and the effect must be forthcoming.
5. REALIZATION—Now is the time of knowing within yourself that the thing you desire is firmly impressed on your subconscious mind. Release the picture and allow the miracle of Macro-Mind Magnetism to take over, directing your subconscious mind power to go to work and bring back the results.

Now, release it and let it go.

MACRO-MIND MOTIVATORS

1. I turn within to the limitless resources of Macrocosmic Mind and I am filled with Light, Wisdom, and Awareness. Success is mine!
2. The Power of Macrocosmic Mind is at work in me and through me to attract to me all that I need to be happy and fulfilled. I am not limited by space or time.

3. Divine Mind always has, Divine Mind always will, supply my every need.
4. I am now in the presence of pure Macrocosmic Mind Power. I am eagerly immersed in Life, Love, and Wisdom. I acknowledge the Presence and Power of Macrocosmic Mind and its activity in my affairs. Its pure substance brings that which I desire into my world, according to perfect Universal Law.
5. Macrocosmic Mind is an Eternal Fountain of rich ideas. I attune my mind with Macrocosmic Mind and these ideas open new channels of supply, and I am prospered.
6. I am enthusiastic and confident. I am ready for the success and prosperity that Macrocosmic Mind has for me.
7. I am enthusiastic and confident. I am ready for the Success and Prosperity that is mine by Divine Right.

2

How Macrocosmic Mind Power Can Help You Control Your Destiny

How Alive Are You?

Although there is in reality only one Macrocosmic Mind—sometimes called Life, Intelligence, Livingness—in the Universe, there is yet a sense in which you are individual or separate, a sense in which you are free to follow your wonderful will, for the Creator did not make puppets! *You are a three-phase being, comprised of SPIRIT, SOUL, AND BODY.* Let's take a closer look at the ingredients blending together to make You!

A. SPIRIT

This aspect of yourself is the *real Macrocosmic idea,* Reality of your being, the Divine Blueprint of life. It is that beautiful spark of life energy from the great Macrocosmic Mind which abides within each one of us. *It is the "Creative Source" of yourself from which comes all that you are.* The *Spirit* part of your being is often called the "Superconscious Mind." From this aspect of yourself, you draw all that is needed to help you grow and express the consciousness of Universal or Macrocosmic Mind, for *Spirit* IS the consciousness of all good, all perfection. It is the I AM THAT I AM—your individuality!

B. SOUL

The soul part of your being is often called your *Subconscious and Conscious Mind. Here is where you amplify the divine Macrocosmic ideas which come to you from the Spirit part of your being.* Your soul is, in a sense, the *vehicle* for the spirit, and a beautiful one it is!

Charles Fillmore, in *The Revealing Word,* describes *Soul* as "Man's consciousness; the underlying idea back of any expression. It is the many accumulated ideas back of his present expression. In its original and true sense, the *Soul* of man is the expressed idea of man in Divine Mind . . . the *Soul* includes the *Conscious* and the *Subconscious* minds. *Soul* makes the body; the *body* is the outer expression of the *Soul;* and bodily health is in exact corespondence to the health of the *Soul.*

"THE UNFOLDMENT OF DIVINE IDEALS IN THE SOUL, OR CONSCIOUSNESS OF MAN, AND THE BRINGING OF THESE IDEALS INTO EXPRESSION IN THE BODY IS SOUL DEVELOPMENT."

C. BODY

Your *Body* is the lovely vehicle through which *Spirit* and *Soul* manifest according to your current understanding and awareness! *It is truly the "temple of the LIVING GOD," for you are God in the embryonic stage.* Instead of seeing *Spirit* and *Soul* inprisoned in your *Body*, you can see the body vehicle beautifully and meaningfully motivated by the Presence and Power of Macrocosmic Mind and visualize yourself as BEING A MAGNIFICENT OUTPICTURING OF DIVINE POTENTIAL! What a fantastic opportunity your body offers you to "let your light shine!"

Question: How alive are you?
Answer: As alive as your awareness allows!

Are you really alive, alert, awake, and enthusiastic about life? Or, are you wearing a mask? When you awakened this morning did you consider yourself unprosperous, unhappy, sick, or unfortunate? You do not have to endure a time of hardship, injustice, or lack. *You do not have to be limited in any way!* These old restrictive thoughts are merely masks covering up the reality of your identity. They are crystallized beliefs that *hold no power over you, except the power you allow them to have.*

When an actor on the stage wears a mask with small openings for the eyes, it is difficult for him to get a broad, comprehensive view of the world about him. Your narrow thoughts are equally limiting in viewing your world. But when you dissolve the mask of personal consciousness through the application in your life of the miracle-working power of Macrocosmic Mind, then you can see yourself in the *true light of being.*

Right now, decide you will arise out of all useless, crystallized beliefs. Discard the masks of doubt and fear, of limitations and bondage, of unhappiness or lack, of insecurity. Old thoughts and conditions cannot hold you, for you are free through the truth you have attained.

When you behold yourself as a divine being, filled with the life, wisdom, and love of Macrocosmic Mind, you are holding to the truth of your Reality. All masks then fall away and the beauty and radiance of your soul sparkles like a shining star.

UNLOCK THE DOOR TO YOUR REAL SELF IMAGE. THROW AWAY YOUR MASK AND BE YOURSELF.!

1. Don't be afraid to be "different"!
2. Lose your fear of so-called "perfect people."
3. Become more spontaneous, letting the real *you* flow forth into your life and affairs.
4. Rely on the Macrocosmic power of yourself.
5. Believe in your divine origin.

There is a story about a miniature deer called the musk deer that lives in and around India. Once a year the glands within that little animal secrete a fragrance. This fragrance is so delightful and intoxicating that these little deer begin to look for it. They become very anxious, running in every direction, searching, only to be turned back when they can't find it. They allow fear to creep in and they panic, and they crash into trees and into bushes. Finally, they rush across the precipice in search of the fragrance and to their own destruction. If only that little deer could realize that what he was searching for came from right within himself!

The Magic Presence Exercise

Many times you become upset and disturbed because various situations seem to approach you from all sides, awaiting your attention. Perhaps you mentally review a hundred times some area of work that needs to be done, when actually you need to think about it only once! It is important then to *train yourself* to meet the demands of the moment *as it comes!* Then, quietly and peacefully go about doing what is necessary. Most people's minds are like a gigantic ragbag, filled with untidy thoughts, desires, and anticipations. How in the world could fresh, inspiring vibrations of thought possibly filter through all that mess! If your mind is stuffed tightly with a conglomeration of odds and ends, the rays of Macrocosmic Light and guidance which might penetrate and assist you are rebuffed.

So clean house! Get out of the habit of worrying, worrying, worrying, over the little pinpricks of life. It's the sword stabs that require attention!

Every atom of your being throbs with active intelligence. The very air you breathe and the world in which you live is truly a-thrill with Divine Intelligence, which seeks to impart to you ALL you wish to know about everything. That same Divine Intelligence will perform wonders for you if you will make contact with it in faith!

There is an exercise called "The Breath of the Magic Presence" which was one of the ancient secret methods used by the mystics, the masters, and by every adept. And it still is used by students of Truth the world over! In this exercise, when faithfully practiced, you will find a method for creating a strong psychic, magnetic, healthy body and mind energized by vitalized, quickened psychic centers.

You will find that this exercise adds greatly to your vitality. The deep breathing gives you an extra amount of *positive energy* which is used by your consciousness in further quickening and enlivening the senses or awareness of those parts of the body on which you are concentrating. The extra amount of vital life force and energy that enters the blood cells of the lungs each time you take a deep breath and hold it, while concentrating, is passed off by the blood in its circulation at those points with an extra amount of vital life force which includes the very essence of spiritual power and consciousness that is required to awaken your spiritual chakras.

The Breath of the Magic Presence

Sit in a chair in a comfortable, relaxed, restful attitude. It is important that you do not feel uncomfortable, tightened, squeezed, or uneasy in any portion of your body. Wear loose clothing. Try to sit where no bright light or loud noise will distract your attention or disturb your thoughts during this special time of spiritual attunement.

Now, begin to concentrate your whole mind, your entire consciousness, upon the bottoms of your feet. *Feel* the skin of your feet against the material of your socks or stockings. Hold this thought for a few seconds as you inhale deeply, hold the breath, and breathe out. Feel the life in the bottoms of your feet, feel the tingle and warmth. Now, move your attention along to your toes. Concentrate all of your mind-consciousness *on just that part of your body* as though it were the only part of you that is alive and active. As you practice the deep breathing, concentrate first on the toes of the left foot, and then the right. See them strong and healthy. Visualize brilliant white light swirling around them, permeating all the atoms and blessing and healing.

Next, continue to hold the vision of this swirling white light and slide your concentration up the foot and concentrate it upon your ankles, first the left and then the right. Feel the bones and your skin against them to some degree. Swirl the light around and see your ankles strong and healthy.

Come upward, now, to the calves of your legs, feeling the aliveness of you until you can feel the pressure of your stockings or pants against your skin. Swirl the light around, seeing it do its perfect work. Next, raise your attention to both knees, first the left and then the right, until you can feel the *throbbing* of the blood vessels, or existence of the bones in the knees, and all your consciousness is centered in these two parts of your body. Bring your consciousness up through your thighs, up to your waist, until you can feel the pressure of your clothes. Remember, as you concentrate to continue with the deep breathing and visualization of swirling light. Feel the clothes you are wearing against your flesh. Feel the presence of the internal organs of your body. Now, slowly raise your consciousness to the chest and breasts, and up to your neck. Release it now.

Rest for a minute or so, then start with your hands, allowing them to lie comfortably in your lap. First concentrate on your fingers, then your wrists, then your elbows, finally arriving at your shoulders. Concentrate your attention now on your heart until you can feel its beating inside your chest. Be aware of your lungs until you are conscious of the rhythm of your breathing. Turn your thoughts to your back, swirling the white light all along the spine, upward to the base of the skull. Concentrate on the lower part of your face until you can feel your teeth resting in your gums. Lift your attention to your nose and eyes, feeling them relaxed. Swirl the light in and around your ears and finally, raise it through the top of your head until you can feel your scalp, the hair upon it, and have a realization of your brain within your scalp. Then, release the light in a golden shower falling all over and around you.

If you will give one full minute of concentration to each part of the body in the manner described, then, begin all over, starting at the feet and flowing to the top of the head, you will experience the best hour you have ever spent.

The idea is to begin at the lower extremities of the body and gradually concentrate, quicken, and *awaken the consciousness in the individual body sections, one at a time*. This causes the blood to become excited and stimulated in these parts. It will also cause the objective brain consciousness, as well as the spiritual consciousness, to increase in that part of the body. Your nerve centers in the different body parts will become awakened by this process until by the time you have reached your head, you will find that your entire body is tingling with life and vitality such as you have not experienced before.

Understanding the Longings of Your Soul

When an artist begins transferring an idea onto a new canvas, at first there may be only a baffling mixture of color and indistinguishable form. Then, as the idea grows into more complete expression, the canvas begins to "live" with the bright colors, the intricate shadings, and the delicate brush strokes that add the finishing touch.

When an office building is in the construction stage, for a period of time a person passing by the construction site will see only the deeply laid foundation and the towering steel skeleton. *There is no visible evidence of what the completed structure will look like.*

If you trace any work from its beginning, you often find that, at first, it goes through a stage of formlessness, a period of seeming nothingness until a semblance of order is produced in the outer form. Then the eye can begin to discern what is happening.

The artist does have a *definite design* in his mind and it emerges in time as a beautiful and often inspiring picture on his canvas. The building contractor is also working according to a plan and it eventually becomes apparent.

Often, we can see periods of seeming formlessness, times of outer confusion in our own life when ideas are in the embryonic stage. Life may then seem chaotic, but what appeared chaotic progressively evolves into a beautiful manifestation. What a comfort is the assurance that we are ever evolving.

YOU ARE THE EVER-RENEWING, EVER-UNFOLDING EXPRESSION OF THE BEAUTIFUL AND INCORRUPTIBLE SPIRIT OF MACROCOSMIC MIND!

Question: What, then, is that unshakable, penetrating, longing stirring in the depths of your soul? It is very real. Sometimes you try to push it aside and pretend it isn't there, but like the persistent boomerang, it comes right back. Why?

Answer: Within every single individual resides a Divine Plan, a Macro-Blueprint, for the unfoldment of your higher spiritual nature. This plan is MACRO-WILL for you, and you must seek to follow it!

As you discover and begin to use the divine ideas that make up your divine plan, you unfold the plan in your own Soul consciousness (mind) and manifest it in your body and affairs. *The real, or true, Self of you is the perfect idea that God has of man. It is the Christ, created in the image and after the likeness of God.* It is the *Spirit* phase of your three-phase nature.

A plan or pattern may be perfect in itself. However, by the time it is produced in outer form there may be many differences in the manifestation, if the one seeking to bring forth the plan or pattern does not follow the details of the blueprint!

THE REAL SELF IS THE DIVINE PATTERN WITHIN EACH OF US, AND IT IS THE SAME CHANGELESS, LIMITLESS NATURE THAT IS GOD.

That which manifests disharmony in mind, body, and affairs occurs when the human consciousness, through lack of understanding of how the Law of Mind Action works, accepts thoughts contrary to the original divine plan. These negative thoughts in turn reproduce like conditions in the mind, body, and affairs.

But this condition can be changed!

> **Affirm: I now let go and put out of my life all adverse thoughts. I am grateful that Macrocosmic Mind is fully established throughout my entire being.**

Determine that your mind and body and affairs are NOW fully attuned to the Omnipotent Presence of Macrocosmic Mind. You will actually *feel* the powerful surge of energy from Macrocosmic Mind!

> **Now affirm: I now know the bliss and satisfaction that springs from the union of my soul with the Living Christ, and that bliss and satisfaction abides in me through all eternity. I know that the power and presence of Macrocosmic Mind is fully established in me, and I am in control of my life and affairs.**

How does a tiny seed grow? First, it is sown in the soil, and that soil can be dry and rocky, sandy, barren, or fertile. As the life force begins to move in the seed, it must first break through the protecting shell. As the life force becomes stronger, the seed germinates and works its way upward through numerous particles of earth before breaking through into the air. Then it must triumph over hot sunlight, drenching rains, and bending winds to grow into the strong, productive plant it has the capability of being.

I think perhaps the greatest goal, the greatest accomplishment that mortal man can have in one lifetime is to find a burning, fiery desire to learn!

The Life That Had a Master Mission

Every person has a mission in life! And *your* mission is unlike that of any other person. It is unique unto you. There is a job to be done, a life-slot to fill that *only you* can fill.

When we look into the lives of some of the world's greatest people, we often find that strong, burning desire to keep on keeping on at whatever their life work depicts. Abraham Lincoln is one of the prime examples of the man who couldn't win—*but did!*

Mr. Lincoln was born February 12, 1809 in a backwoods cabin three miles from Hodgenville, Kentucky. He had little formal education. In fact, it was said that he went to school by "littles"—a little now and a little then! But Abe Lincoln loved to read and *something inside of him stirred the heart in his chest with a fire and determination that was unbreakable or unbeatable.* He experienced many vocations in his search for his life work—he was a rail-splitter, a flatboatman, a store keeper, a postmaster, a surveyor. The story of his younger years reads like a dismal soap opera:

He failed in business in 1831;
Was defeated for the legislature in 1832;
Second failure in business in 1833;
Suffered a nervous breakdown in 1836;
Was defeated for Speaker in 1838;
Was defeated for Elector in 1840;
Was defeated for Congress in 1843;
Was defeated again for Congress in 1848;
Was defeated for Senate in 1855;
Was defeated for Vice President in 1856;
Was defeated for Senate in 1858;
But was elected PRESIDENT in 1860 as the sixteenth president of our nation!

Would *you* have hung on to your goals in the face of such seeming tremendous defeat?

Your Belief About Your Destiny Is Your Belief About Yourself!

The other day, I was talking with Tom C., a young college student, about his future. Tom is a brilliant young man who is tall, good-looking, extremely personable, and his eyes fairly sizzle and dance with enthusiasm and the joy of living. He was on the verge of an exciting new career in music and felt he was standing on the threshhold of his destiny. But he wasn't always so happy. I remembered another day when we had lunch together, about a year ago, when Tom was about as down as a dandelion seed! Dreams and goals had been pouring out of Tom when he suddenly stopped, looked at me, and intently asked, "Rebecca, am I crazy?"

A little startled at the abrupt question, I looked at him and replied, "I don't think so, but why do you ask this question?"

Then Tom told me how all of his life he had experienced the feeling that he had a work to do; that somewhere in this big wide world there was a special place that had his name on it, and he *had* to find his place. He talked about how friends and classmates teased and criticized him when he expressed ideas about his beliefs until, finally, he held his thoughts close within and stopped talking about them!

I then explained to Tom how he was feeling the inner promptings from Macrocosmic Mind, nudging him on toward his destiny in this life experience. I, too, had experienced these same *feelings, and criticisms!* Yet, somehow I simply KNEW at an early age that there was a purpose for my being in embodiment and I was determined to find that purpose. Many doors opened in the early years of my life, and each one was meaningful in the progression of finding my *right place.* Times of discouragement came when the feeling of fulfillment failed to be manifest, but those were the times when I *held on to my belief.* And the realization did come! For me, and for Tom.

The Man Who Had an Outstanding Destiny

Thomas Carlyle heaved a great sigh of relief as he finished writing his great work, *The French Revolution.* This massive manuscript represented two years of the hardest work he had done in his entire life. He had literally poured himself into his work, striving to capture on paper the thought images that rampaged through his brilliant mind. But at last the work was finished, and he bundled up the huge manuscript and took it to a close friend, John Stuart Mill, for Mr. Mill's personal evaluation.

Several days passed, and one morning a rap came at the door. Thomas Carlyle walked to the door in great strides, eager to learn his friend's thoughts about this new work. As he opened the door, he came face to face with a John Stuart Mill whose face was chalky white and actually looking ill.

"What on earth happened?" Mr. Carlyle asked as he pulled his friend into the house. The words then tumbled out of his mouth like a flood as Mr. Mill told Mr. Carlyle that his maid had used the bundle of papers that was the manuscript to start a fire, not knowing what precious fuel she used!

Thomas Carlyle was disgruntled and distraught. For days he paced the floor, back and forth, ranting and raving at the fate that would do such a dastardly thing to him. *Two years of his life had simply gone up in smoke!* What was he going to do? He had poured *everything* into this work and now he was drained. There was nothing more left inside. He couldn't recapture the fire and the feeling and knowledge that had flowed into his original work. He shook his head in despair as he gave in to despondency.

Thomas Carlyle then began to spend long hours at an upstairs bedroom window, staring bleakly into the nothingness he felt. One morning, as he stood dejectedly gazing out the window across the rooftops, a flicker of movement caught his attention. He focused his eyes toward the movement and noticed a brick mason preparing to lay the bricks for a wall. Mr. Carlyle watched. Brick by brick, the mason worked, gently and lovingly spreading the mortar and laying each brick individually in place. As Mr. Carlyle watched throughout the day, he saw a beautiful decorative and serviceable brick wall taking shape as the brick mason patiently continued his work.

Suddenly, the idea struck Thomas Carlyle's mind like a flash of lightening—just as patience, persistence, and singleness of purpose could erect a brick wall, so would he reconstruct his work of *The French Revolution!*

Peace came at last to his mind and ideas began to flow again. Thomas Carlyle pushed aside seeming defeat and began again on what has become the most colossal work of his lifetime. His own understanding had increased in leaps and bounds and was reflected in a new and greater version, giving the world a work that far surpassed the original.

Yes, brick by brick, word by word, thought by thought, dream by dream, we build the substance from which the masterpieces of our lives are produced. Remember, though, that a brick mason puts together bricks which someone else has made, while one who is truly inspired is a creator, putting together something new, beautiful, and meaningful!

You Are Greater than You Think!

You are one of the most unique and intelligent manifestations of life on earth! *You already have within you the greatest reservoir of untapped potential and creative power imaginable; the greatest portion of which you have yet to use!*

This reality is true of every single human being. The Macrocosmic Power which flows through you is impersonal, yet you can make it very personal, according to the manner in which you use it. If you use it intelligently and wisely, it will be your great benefactor.

THINK BIG! *Stretch your fantastic mind!* You have been given a variety of gifts—spiritual, mental, and physical. Seek an enlightened perception of your true self so you may develop your skills and abilities. Put constructive ideas to work; use ideas that will *transform your life!*

It's time that you catch a mighty vision of your God-Self, of your own divine powers, and *make use* of these God-given powers.

> **Affirm: I discover and make effective use of my God-given powers.**

Enjoy being yourself! Use the following exercise in self-awareness, acceptance, and appreciation. I offer it to you without comment or explanation, knowing that your consciousness determines your acceptance, rejection, modification, and/or expansion of the activity described.

> **I enjoy being myself. I enjoy being myself spiritually. I enjoy being myself emotionally. I enjoy being myself mentally. I enjoy being myself verbally. I enjoy being myself silently. I enjoy being myself physically. I enjoy being myself internally. I enjoy being myself externally. I enjoy being myself in time and space. I enjoy being myself eternally. I am happy! I enjoy being ______________________________. I enjoy**
> **(fill in blank space with your own name)**
>
> **being myself in my special assignment on this radiant planet earth. I enjoy being myself in my work, my relationships with people, in my times of rest and relaxation, in all my activities. I enjoy being myself in my growing consciousness of my eternal nature. I enjoy being myself in all the changes that my growing consciousness necessarily brings into my life and affairs.**

I enjoy being myself, so it is only natural that I enjoy letting, urging, and encouraging you to be yourself. It's great to be alive and well and enjoying yourself!

Why Courage Is the Only Remedy for Fear

Everyone can improve himself regardless of his situation, place in life, or circumstances. But it is necessary to prove to yourself that by your own thoughts and actions you have the power to *accomplish all that which you make up your mind to do.*

How many times have you been on "rock-bottom" and some kind words and thoughts of encouragement spoken by a friend lifted you up and made you feel like a person again? It is your divine birthright to express yourself as a healthy, happy, prosperous person. *Yet, it is impossible for you to express your true inner self as long as you are fearful instead of courageous.*

Oh, how I want to impress upon you that courage, *real courage,* is a spiritual idea stemming from Macrocosmic Mind! When you desire courage with all the intensity of your heart, believe in it, and demand it until it becomes a part of your nature, then you are fearless, dauntless, gallant, bold, and brave.

> FEAR IS ONE OF THE MOST SUBTLE AND DESTRUCTIVE ERRORS THAT THE MIND OF MAN EXPERIENCES.

Fear is a paralyzer of mental action; it weakens both mind and body. Fear throws dust in your eyes and hides the mighty spiritual forces of Macrocosmic Mind that are always with you. Truly blessed are those who deny fear and ignorance and affirm the Presence and Power of Macrocosmic Mind.

I have known of people who would take tranquilizer pills to eliminate feelings of fear; but what happens when the effects of those pills wears off? The person still has to face the same situations and feelings as before, and the situation often intensifies. Yet, when you *reach the realization that nothing has any power to harm you, and when you can imagine yourself as courageous and believe that you are courageous, your Subconscious Mind will go to work to make this belief a reality.*

How Precognition Saved a Life

Vera L. ran a hand across her brow as she cleared the breakfast dishes from the table. She couldn't shake the oppressive, uncomfortable feeling that had been brewing since the day before. It was one of those weird things that you couldn't really put your finger on.

This feeling was somewhat alleviated as excitement and youthful enthusiasm filled the atmosphere during breakfast. Her teenage daughter and some friends were discussing their projects for the day. They wanted to involve Sondra, Vera's three-year-old granddaughter, in their plans but Vera emphatically turned thumbs-down on the request. For some reason, she didn't want to let the child get too far away from her watchful eye.

The day progressed and all was peaceful and calm. Sondra was put to bed for an afternoon nap and had been asleep for about thirty minutes. Wanting to check on Sondra, Vera tiptoed to the bedroom and peeked in. Her heart leaped, and she gasped as she saw the small child struggling silently to breathe. Sondra's face was chalky white and her little body was bathed in perspiration; yet no sounds came from her throat. Vera snatched up the telephone and dialed the emergency squad to come at once. Then, she ran into the bathroom and wet a bathcloth with cold water and rushed back to bathe Sondra's face.

At that point all Vera could do was pray. In a matter of minutes the rescue squad was at the door, had placed the tiny body on a stretcher in the ambulance, and was enroute to the hospital.

Then came the time of waiting and uncertainty. Several hours passed before the verdict arrived—a severe attack of spinal meningitis! Sondra was in a coma and seemingly paralyzed! Vera called her daughter-in-law, and then went into the hospital chapel. She tried to remember what her daughter-in-law had said about the power of the mind being so fantastic. It had something to do with the thought that no situation was so great or intense or small that it couldn't be helped.

Vera thought about Sondra, and began to silently repeat, "*You now are healed!*" For three days Sondra lay in the coma with a raging fever. Vera held on to the thought, "*You now are healed!*" Finally, on the morning of the fourth day, Sondra's fever subsided, and she awakened by sitting immediately upright in the hospital bed with the remark, "I'm hungry!"

The doctor said the family had experienced a miracle. Sondra remained in the hospital for twelve days to be certain her health was fully restored. Vera had tears in her eyes as she told me, "Never again will I doubt the tremendous power of man's mind working in alignment with God-Mind!"

Why a Rich, Full Life Is Important to You

No person is born happy. Happiness is not a gift, nor can it be purchased in any of the markets of the world. *Happiness is a state of mind which must be achieved, striven for, and built out of your own life experiences.* Yet, happiness is the dream of every person on earth, and most people's dream of happiness includes a rich, full life.

THE PRIMARY REASON WHY YOU DESIRE HAPPINESS, WHY YOU DESIRE TO HAVE A RICH, FULL LIFE IS BECAUSE YOU ARE A MARVELOUS CREATION CALLED A HUMAN BEING AND YOU ARE ENDOWED WITH A MAGNIFICENT LIFE PLAN AND THE FANTASTIC, EXCEPTIONAL POWERS WITH WHICH TO FULFILL THAT LIFE PLAN!

As example, think of the family cat! Its day consists of lapping bowls of milk, enjoying the food placed in front of it, stretching out to nap in a warm, sunny spot. That cat lives by animal instinct and has merely the ability to purr or stretch or scratch, to bring forth kittens if it is a female, to live the life plan assigned to cats. But YOU, *superior creation that you are,* have been abundantly blessed with many gifts, some of the greatest being the power of free will, of judgement, and of determination. *You have the ability to make of yourself anything you desire to be!*

When you stretch forward in life and reach for the desires of your heart, you take the first important steps toward making something really great of yourself. Not only will you reap untold benefits for your decision, but you will also be an inspiration to others who will admire and respect you and your ability, and what you have made of yourself.

Haven't you been in a room filled with people when some man or woman entered the room and instantly the atmosphere became charged with supervitality? Have you wondered why this happened? When you are holding true to your goals, and living true to yourself, a feeling of confidence and poise flows from you which is unmistakably felt by others close by. Your very presence among other people inspires them to do the same things in their life—take control!

I'm sure there will be those who say, "Well, if he or she can be so successful, I can too!" That intuitive voice inside always offers encouragement. The pseudo-scientist may shrug and say, "If you can't see it and measure it, it doesn't exist," or "If you can't put a label on it, it isn't for real!" Fiddlesticks!

The average person today is still trying to determine the difference between intellect and intuition. I sometimes wonder if primitive man was perhaps in some ways better off—*he knew the difference, and he depended fully on his intuition, the voice of Macrocosmic Mind whispering to him, rather than on his memory bank.* Usually we listen first to our logical mind or intellect, which is really a great memory bank of stored past experiences which are constantly recalled to determine our response to any stimulation, mental or otherwise. Yet, how do you live fully *alive* in the present moment if you are imprisoned by the dead past?

It sometimes takes "blood, sweat, and tears" to break through the strong bondage of the human intellect and become willing to listen quietly to our inner connection with the cosmos. But like the gentle kiss of a soft summer breeze, this guidance caresses our minds with truth and we continue to travel forward to our soul's desires.

Twelve Ways to Find Happiness

An ancient legend tells of a fair maiden who was offered a rare gift by a wealthy king. This king presented her with a large velvet bag filled with pearls with the promise that she could keep the largest, most perfect pearl she could find in the bag as her very own.

However, three conditions were established. First, she must choose only one pearl; second, she must remove one pearl at a time from the bag and either accept it or reject; and third, once a pearl was rejected, she could not pick it up again for a second look!

Excitedly, the maiden began taking pearls from the velvet bag. She pulled forth many large, beautiful, and near perfect pearls. But she kept looking for that one special pearl which would be just a little larger, just a little more lustrious, just a little more perfect. Therefore, she passed up many nearly perfect treasures.

As the maiden delved deeper into the bag, the pearls became smaller and of poorer quality. Occasionally she found, not a beautiful pearl, but a pebble. Now, inasmuch as she couldn't go back and claim one of the pearls she had formerly discarded she had to continue looking into the bag, and the pearls became smaller and more common. When, at last, she reached the bottom of the velvet bag, nothing was left except a few pebbles and she went away as empty-handed as she came.

So it is with many of us. We rush through life, trying to find a better this and a better that, completely missing the abundance of today. We should stop, decide what we really want, and accept its manifestation in our life.

You see, the things we are looking FOR, we are looking WITH. We can find and experience good only to the extent that we embody a mental image of that which we so greatly desire.

We have the priceless pearls of life right in front of us to claim as our very own, and we don't have to sell all that we have in order to attain happiness. Let's look at some ways we can be happy.

1. COUNT YOUR BLESSINGS! Old and trite perhaps, but nevertheless absolutely true. Yet, every atom of the universe responds to praise and thanksgiving. Our gratitude and appreciation of life itself, the world in which we live, and the manifold blessings God gives each of us, is an essential part of true happiness.

2. BE LOVABLE! Every single person needs love, but how many of us are really lovable? As we become more lovable ourselves, we attract more love into our lives from others and it grows outward in ever-widening circles. When we love God first, then He who IS Love can help us be more lovable.

3. ACT MATURELY! Grow up a little more every day. Learn the meaningful lessons life offers, but wear the learning lightly. It has been said that we must "put away childish things" but this doesn't mean we lose the childlike simplicity of those who are truly "children of a king!"

4. REMEMBER TO WHOM YOU BELONG! Realize that you are a most important part of God's plan! You are a unique link in the great human chain that extends from creation into the unknowable future. Never again will an "aggregate of atoms" just like you be in attendance on this planet earth!

5. REFUSE TO BE AFRAID! Life is filled with too much fear—of ourselves, of others, of what we regard as being "cut off" from God, and of a world of unknown terrors. *Fear thwarts happiness!* Fear is the most destructive of all human emotions, even surpassing jealousy in its corrosiveness!

6. STAY HEALTHY AND FIT! A simple remedy perhaps, but to be truly happy, you must be in good health. People who are sincerely happy tend to become ill less often, have fewer aches and pains, and recover more quickly from an illness that might sneak up on them. A happy person seems to age more slowly, have better digestion, clearer skin, better carriage, more normal circulation—I could go on and on.

7. TAKE TIME TO ENJOY LIFE! When I think of this thought, I think of the slogan, "going nowhere in a hurry!" How much more we get out of life when we take the time to enjoy it to the fullest degree. What a good rewarding feeling it is to simply stand and stare at something beautiful. Remember that serenity is never in a rush, never impatient, never lacking enough time to do that which needs to be done. George Louis Palmella said, "Happiness is like time and space—we make and measure it ourselves; it is as fancy, as big, as little, as you please; just a thing of contrasts and comparisons."

8. STAY ALERT! Sharpen your wits! A keen mind and a sharp intellect will stay the ravages of old age. Look at things in a light manner; in fact, why not give situations *the light touch* instead of heavy-handed pessimism.

9. LIVE USEFULLY NOW! Look around you. Life has so much to offer, and you have so much to give. And you can live usefully in the little things of life as well as in the great and noble sacrifices. Sweeping a floor, making a bed, watering a plant, cooking a meal can all be accomplished in an attitude of giving God the glory. Living usefully means seeing through one another and seeing one another through!

10. GIVE OF YOURSELF! It is impossible for anyone to live happily completely unto himself. It is only normal for us to want to give of ourselves and of what we have—our love, our service, our devotion, our help, our praise, our friendship, our encouragement of another, or plain and simple ordinary kindness. The quicker you respond to this inner part of your being, the sooner you will achieve happiness.

11. VALUE SIMPLICITY! How we need to rediscover simplicity. Truth is simple. Life, in reality, is simple. Most of the time the simple pleasures are the best pleasures. Love and goodness, although not necessarily valued in our sophisticated, "advanced technology," are still the best sources of happiness.

12. WELCOME LIFE'S CHANGES! Nature's inexorable law requires that all things must either progress or perish. Nothing ever stays exactly the same. Nature abhors a vacuum and detests the static. Recognizing this truth, we can never find much happiness in our world if we resist and fear change. Welcome change with the positive thought that it will be for the better. You wouldn't want to take any one particular moment of your life and live it continuously forever. Even the joyous and happy times would become boring after awhile. Accept change as a beautiful part of your life. Without it, you might be still wearing animal skins and living in caves!

So, light up your face with a smile of happiness. It is the special glow in the window of your face that tells everyone your heart is at home!

A New Concept That Worked Wonders

Have you thought very much about the power of *visualization?* The art of visualization is like obtaining a large blank canvas, having all the painting materials provided, and you, as the artist, painting your heart's desire in vivid, living color on that canvas! *There is absolutely nothing wrong with desiring to receive something and visualizing its manifestation into your life.* Material things do exist to be used and enjoyed and to think otherwise is to give power to an attitude of lack. And if you believe in and give power to an attitude of lack, then you're not going to get what you desire!

Put your power of Macrocosmic Mind to work. Set it into action to draw whatever you desire to you. There are many things you could desire: a color television, a new car, a new set of matched luggage, a new watch, a new home, new home furnishings, photography equipment, or ski equipment. These things all exist, you know, and you can draw them to you—and more—by *believing* you will receive them.

Paul V. really wanted a new color television set. However, he had just finished three years of professional training and was just getting started in a new position in a new geographical location. Paul knew his good job would provide ample finances for the things he wanted within a reasonable time as soon as he recouperated from his training expenses. But he really wanted a television set *now*!

Being aware of the power of Macrocosmic Mind and the tremendous attracting magnetism of *visualization*, he decided to manifest a color television set!

Every evening, Paul would sit in his favorite chair, relax, close his eyes, and think of a nice color television set. He thought about all the pleasure the set would bring, the ball games he would watch, the friends he would invite over to share an evening's programing with him. He visualized a nice 21-inch portable set that would fit just perfectly in the corner of his living room which had been dubbed "TV Corner." Paul also visualized a nice wood table for the television set to rest on, with storage space underneath. He made a mental picture of the television set in his imagination and saw it coming to him, easily, perfectly. He claimed a nice color television set as his own and BELIEVED it would be coming to him presently. Paul didn't know how his desire would manifest, and *it didn't matter*, he simply knew with absolute certainty it would come. For ten minutes every day Paul held this visualization and then released it and went about his work.

A month passed. Then, one day Paul received a telephone call from a couple who had been his friends for several years. They were moving into a new house and their television set (which they had purchased only a year previously) didn't fit in with the new decor. They remembered that Paul didn't have one and called him saying that if he would come to pick it up, the television set was his!

Paul thanked them graciously and made arrangements to pick up the set the next day. When he arrived at their home, it was an effort to restrain his joyful surprise. *The set they gave him was a 21-inch color portable, name brand, beautiful set, and the wooden table they also gave him was exactly as he had pictured in his visualization!*

If Paul could manifest a color television set through using the power of Macrocosmic Mind, *SO CAN YOU!* You may not desire a television set, but *the principle works,* whatever your desire.

Master Training Techniques

The only thing in the Garden of Life that grows fast is a weed! It takes longer for the rose bush to grow, but look at its product! The mighty oak tree takes a decade to grow, but no storm, no blast of wintry earth can shake it down. For the longer a thing takes to grow, the deeper go down the roots into the soil so that no matter what happens above the soil, the thing will not be uprooted.

You are the Master of your life. No matter what it is that you want in life, *you already have the means to obtain it.* Of course, if you never want something, then you shall never have it. The "*want to have*" means that you have your desire inside already.

A person who has no hands does not want gloves; only the person with hands wants gloves. And because he has hands already, he will have those gloves. This means that there is no wishful thinking in wanting something beyond your present reach. This means there are no fanciful daydreams, hoping for something and then not being able to have your desire. Remember, *when a person wants something, this means he already has it!*

Get this truth so strongly imbedded into your conscious and subconscious mind that it becomes a living, breathing, active part of your soul. Start now on the path to obtaining your desires. Use the following *Master Training Techniques* and YOU SHALL BE MASTER OF YOUR LIFE.

1. *Pinpoint your primary goal in life.*
   Set your mind on what you want. Regardless of what it is that you want in life, you already have the means to obtain it. I can't repeat that fact too often! Order is the thought for the day and first things come first! Set the target! Pinpoint your goal! Establish your desire, and it WILL become a reality. That which you can conceive of, believe in, and

confidently *expect* for yourself, must, according to Universal Law, *become your experience!*

2. *Use Your Imagination Faculty to Fan the Flame of Desire!*
   There's no point in establishing a goal in life unless you *really want it tremendously*. If you don't care, you won't get there! The results you achieve will be in direct proportion to the completeness of your imagery. Remember, BE SPECIFIC!
3. *Be Willing to Give in Order to Get What You Want!*
   Big goals require big efforts. The thing to do is set the goal, regardless of how enormous it may seem, and then start working toward it one detail, one specific, at a time.
4. *Send Correct Signals to Your Subconscious Mind.*
   Remember that the Subconscious Mind is a fantastic computer which has to be properly programmed. If your input is junk, the outcome will also be junk. And there's enough junk hanging around. Besides, you don't need it in your life.
5. *Know How to Accept Defeat–Temporarily.*
   There's no such thing as failure. There is simply unfinished work. Perhaps someone stopped before completing his dream. If this happened to you, then pick up where you left off, or begin again, but *keep trying*.
6. *Believe the Power of Your Thought Can Change Your Life!*
   One of the most powerful forces in the world is a divine idea that has taken root and is sprouting in a human mind. Scriptures even tell us that "If ye have faith, Nothing shall be impossible unto you." (Matt. 17:20.)
7. *See Yourself As You Really Are!*
   Stop looking and thinking of yourself as a scrawny worm that has crawled out of the ground and *start seeing yourself from God's viewpoint*. You're a child of the Universe, a creation of MACROCOSMIC MIND. You are important, and just what gives you the right to go around proclaiming your unimportance?
8. *Be Flexible–God Has Many Doors!*
   Progress invites many alternatives. As you move toward your goal, your perspective may change. The important thing for you to do is to keep your eye on the final picture. Make the art of prosperous thinking a part of your daily life.

Make the "success attitude" a daily habit. Your mind makes up your life, but you are the only one who can make up your mind!

MACRO-MIND "DESTINY" MOTIVATORS

1. I now unlock the door to my real self-image. I throw away the mask of limitations and dare to be myself.
2. Each day as I exercise, I breathe in the pure, vitalizing energy of Macrocosmic Mind; hold the breath to the count of eight; then, slowly release it, breathing out all impurities and all that I no longer desire as a part of me.
3. I am the ever-renewing, ever-unfolding expression of the beautiful and incorruptible Spirit of Macrocosmic Mind.
4. What you are right now and the attributes you have right now are the result of your use or misuse of the magnetic power of your own mind tapping the Universal Power of Macrocosmic Mind.
5. Right use of your mind energy will attract to you health, wealth, and happiness. Incorrect use of your mind energy will attract to you illness, poverty, and unhappiness.
6. I believe in my abilities. I believe I can do anything I make up my mind to do. Right now and forever, I believe I have the power to attract all the good things of life and be happy.
7. I am fearless and brave; I am bold and aggressive. It is impossible for me to be afraid. I am courageous in my thoughts. I am courageous in my feelings. I am courageous in my actions. This is the truth about me.

3

How Macro-Mind Power Can Help You Claim Your Birthright Of Infinite Prosperity

The Law of the Magic Lamp

Almost everyone is familiar with the story of Aladdin and his wonderful lamp. A marvelous genie lived in the lamp who eagerly awaited Aladdin's bidding. Yet, in the story, the genie didn't simply appear whenever Aladdin wished her to appear. He had to *do something* to invoke the genie's presence—*rub the lamp!* When Aladdin took the necessary steps for putting in order that which had been placed in his custody, his good appeared. *This same activity is true for you!*

Rub Your Lamp!

Start right now to use the attributes you already possess, whether they are talents and abilities, material possessions now owned, or fantastic opportunities for service to yourself and to others. *Do the most you know how to do with what you have to do with!*

Take one step at a time; and begin by taking the step *immediately ahead of you.* Use what you already have to good advantage. *Rub your lamp!* Clear the way in your consciousness and in your affairs for the abundant good you earnestly desire.

It's amazing that when you peruse the miraculous demonstrations of prosperity recounted in the Old and New Testaments, you recognize that simple, everyday things are used. For example, David slew the giant, Goliath, with a small pebble hurled from a sling shot! Elijah called forth great abundance to meet a widow's daily needs by using the small amount of oil she had in her house!

Jacob won a superb dower from his father-in-law, Laban, by intelligently using some spotted willow sticks! Joseph mastered his dungeon experience in Egypt and became an "overnight" success as second in command to Pharoah. Jesus broke five loaves and two fishes and fed a multitude of five thousand persons. And I could go on and on. All these people had one thing in common:

> THEY PROVED THAT ANY PICTURE HELD FIRMLY IN MIND MUST COME FORTH AS A RESULT IN ITS OWN WAY AND IN ITS OWN TIME!

I've heard people say that they have been unable to succeed in demonstrating greater prosperity in their lives because they haven't had the same opportunities as someone else. *Ridiculous!* It's true, everyone isn't born with the proverbial "silver spoon" in his mouth, benefiting as the offspring of fantastically wealthy parents. Yet, everyone can go out and obtain the desired opportunities. *It's there for you if you want it!*

We sometimes get in the rut of thinking that miracles are "mysterious" and must come through totally unexpected channels. This is erroneous thinking. In reality, miracles are events that take place as a result of the operation of a higher, unknown law. All true action is governed by Universal Laws. Nothing just *happens* haphazardly! All happenings are the result of cause and can be explained under the Law of Cause and Effect. Miracles are actually built on simple things, greatly imbued and impregnated with *faith*!

If You Think You Can; You Can!

This truth was deeply impressed upon me through an experience in my own life. Since early childhood, a strong, undeniable urge to write lived as closely as my shadow. While a sophomore in high school, I wrote my first book! It was about something I loved greatly at the time—*horses*—and I poured my loving thoughts and feelings on reams of paper. Of course, the English teacher gave me a fantastic grade and loads of encouragement. Enthusiasm soared. I wrote steadily and profusely. Probably a lot of what I was writing was mediocre in quality, but *it was so much better than I had realized I could do* that it seemed as though a miracle was happening. And indeed it was!

I continued writing. Several years passed. Ideas for "happy" articles began pouring through my mind. I could look at the humorous side of life and write about it. From the recesses of my mind came age-old wisdom—do something more than simply write; do something *with* what you write! *Rub the lamp!* I took action.

Bold as brass; and with more courage than "good sense," I walked into the local newspaper office one morning and proclaimed I wanted to write free-lance articles for the paper. Believing in being prepared, I produced four sample articles and submitted them to the editor. In stunned amazement at the intrusion into his office, he stated at me, then reached out took the articles, and read them! My ideas were certainly different from the "blood and guts" usually found in a daily paper. Mr. C., the editor, looked at me and I calmly looked back at him. He shook his head and said, "We don't run this type of article. Now, if you want a job as a reporter, you've got it!"

"No," I replied, "I want to be a *writer,* not a reporter." I closed my mouth and continued looking at him. I visualized him surrounded in dazzling white light and I saw mentally my articles in print each week and bringing lots of favorable comments from his readers, which would help his paper greatly.

After about five minutes, and a lot of paper-shuffling on his desk, he heaved a deep sigh and said, "O.K., tell you what. We will experiment! We will accept your articles on a weekly basis. You will submit the articles one week in advance and, if accepted, you will have an article published every Thursday evening."

"Will I have a byline?"

"Why not! The whole idea's crazy anyway!"

Two weeks later my articles began appearing in the newspaper. Within a month, exciting letters were flowing into the editorial office from people who looked forward to reading "some good news" in Thursday evening's paper. I continued to write the byline column for two years and, in addition, wrote several full-page "specials" and included pertinent photographs. (I took my own pictures and was paid additionally for the photography!)

So, you see, the Law of the Lamp really works! But it is important for us to rub our lamps in order for the genie to appear!

Preparing for Prosperity

I've often heard the statement:

WHAT WE ARE IS GOD'S GIFT TO US:
WHAT WE BECOME IS OUR GIFT TO GOD!

I like that statement. We are given energy and vision by Macrocosmic Mind. When these two faculties are used together in a working relationship, the results are success, prosperity, good health, harmony.

Look around you. The world is filled with people who want more and better things, but what are they doing to attain them? Many are "saving" their greater efforts, their more jubilant enthusiasm, their higher amibitions for the "big opportunity" they feel they deserve, but which will never come unless they take action!

Now is the time to give your best efforts! While training in Seminary, I was told by a faculty member, "Never save your best lecture for the right time. Make every time you speak to a group of people the right time! Give the best you have inside at that moment and fulfill that special need of the moment. If you do this, your church will soon overflow because the people will be so eager to hear what you have to say that they will not want to miss a single meeting. They will recognize you are giving your best to them and to their needs."

This faculty member spoke knowingly for he told me his story:

"I had visions of a large congregation in a big, beautiful church, supported by a prosperous treasury. However, my congregation was small; we held our meetings in a rented house; and the weekly offerings barely met urgent needs. I was called away on a leave of absence to go on a lecture tour and was gone from the pastorate for several months.

"One day, I received an urgent call from a devoted member of the little congregation imploring me to return before all was lost. I did, only to find that the modest group I left had become almost extinct, and a generally forlorn atmosphere pervaded the place.

"My first reaction was toward despondency. Then, I remembered—don't react, *act!* I looked about, seeing a shadowy vision of my dream of a perfect work. Suddenly a ray of light blasted into my dark thoughts. 'And I, if I be lifted up, will draw all men unto me.'

"Of course, the answer was right there in my mind all the time—Macro-Mind Power! And I affirmed to myself:

> **"I will accept the dream of greater prosperity. I will accept the dream of large, enthusiastic crowds. I will accept the dream of an appropriate, beautiful building. I will accept the Macro-Vision of tremendous growth for all these dreams are mine to claim, right now, and I claim them!"**

Going forward from that moment in the strength of his Macro-Vision, the work began to grow. Members who had fallen away for various reasons felt drawn back into the congregation. An invigorating spirit of love and growth flowed into the work and it prospered. The forlorn atmosphere was replaced by feelings of enthusiasm and excitement, peace and harmony.

You, too, can prepare for your prosperity by *holding the vision* of beautiful and meaningful things. *Believe* this vision can be a reality, and *take whatever steps are necessary* toward transforming your vision into your actuality. When unexpected, exciting, and happy events occur, I've heard people remark, "Oh, that's just too good to be true!" Wouldn't it be better to express, *"Wow! That's good enough to be true!"* for truly, Macro-Vision and Macro-Mind Power always exceed our greatest understanding of their outworking.

Your Four-Week Macro-Prosperity Diet

Seldom are you able to perceive every step in the way toward the fulfillment of your dreams. You have the energy; and you have the dream, what may be missing are the many steps between the dream and its fulfillment.

The purpose of the Prosperity Diet is *to establish the absolute and unfailing activity of the Law of Cause and Effect in your life.* IF YOU TRULY WANT TO BE PROSPEROUS, YOU CAN BE! Here we go!

FIRST WEEK—*Allow no negative thoughts or attitudes about any lack of supply to reside in your mind.*

Maintain the awareness that your Macro-Vision works Consciously as well as Superconsciously and Subconsciously. Don't underestimate *your* power of *decision.* Decide to change your direction in life or alter any negative attitudes of thoughts, *and you will.* As soon as you make a clear-cut decision and abide by it, you are on your way. From that moment forward your soul energies and Macro-Powers begin working in harmony. Life takes on a new dimension and becomes more worth living. Your creative ideas flow freely and fantastic new energy pours through your body and mind. It might seem difficult at first, but hang in there! You can make it!

Thoughts are like ants. A single ant may annoy you, but you can easily brush it off and it does you no harm. But let yourself fall asleep on an anthill where a thousand ants have the opportunity to swarm over you, and you will certainly wish you had been more careful where you laid yourself down!

SECOND WEEK—*Allow no words regarding shortages, inflation, depression, or lack of any kind come from your lips.*

Also, refuse to listen to words of this category from others. When you speak words of truth with authority, you take conscious control of the good you wish to experience in your life. *All words are formative, but not all words are creative.* Your words are the tremendous vehicles through which your ideas make themselves manifest. Your words have within them the realization of perfect, everywhere-present, always-present magnetic MACRO-POWER. Your words are dominant in restoration of health, wealth, and happiness. This week, take a prosperity vow of watching your words, thereby causing them to work *for* you, not *against* you.

THIRD WEEK—*Allow no appearance of lack to find a home with you.*

Don't put a limit or a time label on your prosperity. If a wealthy person gave you a blank check—certified, so you knew it was valid—and told you to fill it out for whatever amount you desired, what sum would you use? $1,000 . . . $10,000 . . . $100,000 . . . a million dollars . . . or more? To what far-reaching limits of abundance would your dreams fly?

Macro-Mind has given you a blank check on which you can write your heart's desire. You are free to fill in the amount and the kind of payment you want. You have the secret. Know this truth, and when you fill in your check, use Macro-Vision!

FOURTH WEEK—*Feel prosperous; look prosperous; act prosperous.*

You create your own prosperity! Prosperity is based on the conscious possession of the idea of Macro-Abundance back of all things. Situations and circumstances may come and go, but the idea of abundance endures.

> PROSPERITY IS A CONTINUING EXPERIENCE IN PEACE, HEALTH, AND PLENTY. DO YOU DARE TO GO THE LIMIT AND BE TOTALLY OPEN AND RECEPTIVE TO ALL YOUR GOOD?

As you gather unto yourself the abundance that is yours for the taking, prepare for an even greater flow of prosperity that is on its way. Once you get the ball rolling, it's like the proverbial snowball; it increases with every turn.

Feel prosperous —Feel the good of the Universe flowing to you now.

Look prosperous—You are a beautiful human being. You have attributes that can be emphasized in many ways. Utilize what you have in the best manner possible.

Act prosperous —Let your words and actions be those of one who is in tune with the flow of the universe.

If you will follow this Prosperity Diet for the four prescribed weeks, marvelous changes and increases will be occurring in your life and affairs.

> BE DELIBERATE ABOUT PROSPERITY,
> SO PROSPERITY CAN BE DELIBERATE ABOUT YOU!

How Dan K. Used the Macro-Prosperity Diet to Overcome Bankruptcy and Start a New Business

Dan K. was just about as down as anyone could get. His wife had been ill; his work had not unfolded as he wished; bills had accumulated to the point that the only way out of the whole mess Dan could see was to file bankruptcy, and he really couldn't afford to do that! About that time, Dan lost his job with the real estate firm and truly, the bottom fell out of his life. He filed bankruptcy and sat around in gloomy despair.

An opportunity came to have lunch with Dan and we talked about his situation and I told him about the miracle of Macrocosmic Mind and how he could turn his life around. At first he refused to believe his life could ever again be prosperous and good. Yet, something clicked inside of him and said "Yes!" As a starter, I gave him the Macro-Prosperity Diet. "But it looks so easy," Dan remarked.

"Yes, but try it. It isn't quite as easy as it looks, but *it does work!*"

Several months later Dan called and there was a lift to his voice. "Hey, this thing works! You got any more advice?" Then I told him about using the MACRO-VISION technique for visualizing the good he wanted to come into his life. He began to get enthusiastic, for Dan had long had a dream of putting his talent for photography to use in a vocational way.

Almost a year passed, and one day the telephone rang and Dan was jubilant. "Are you going to be home this afternoon?"

"Yes."

"Great, I'm bringing by something for you to see."

When Dan burst through my front door that afternoon, he clutched in his hand a copy of a real estate magazine and thrust it toward me. It was really nicely done and looked interesting. The idea had come to Dan to start a magazine of real estate listings for the real estate firms in the city where he lived. He took action steps to make this idea a reality. After covering most of the city's real estate firms, he had contracts for two pages! He despaired, but remembering some of his Macro-Mind training, he went into the living room and sat quietly visualizing again a beautiful magazine, with many pages, offering help for many people.

As he sat quietly holding the visualization of this desire, the telephone rang. Dan answered, and the call was from a real estate firm wanting to place a full-page advertisement in his magazine. That telephone call was like a turning point. Dan's excitement flowed again. The new page was like a sign from the universe that his dream could come true. The next day he went out to call on potential customers and returned home that night with nine new pages of ads.

Dan's magazine is now the best magazine of its type in the area. His work is flowing, and it's a work he *enjoys* doing. The last time I saw him, Dan told me that his work is now expanding into another city and a third potential city is looking at his work. He told me that in the past month he had deposited $30,000 in his checking account! It was a long way from the day of bankruptcy of *just one year ago.* Dan's future looks bright and I know that from this moment on, Macro-Mind Power is his partner!

Startling Secrets About Prosperity!

Perhaps one of the most startling secrets about prosperity is the truth that it lies *right within yourself.* Once you can recognize this, you have found the master key to open all doors to increased abundance.

Let's look at some other doors:

1. *Prosperity is closer than you think. In fact, it is what you think!* What you can conceive, you can achieve! Your world is affected by your thoughts and feelings much more than you presently realize.
2. *The basic prosperity law states, "Give and you will receive."* Nature abhors a vacuum and will rush to fill it. Give of yourself, your time, your energy, your substance, your material possessions, and open the amazing channels of prosperity to an omnipresent flow into your life.
3. *Keep your desires to yourself!* The reason for this is cosmic. There is absolutely no need to dissipate all the marvelous energy you've generated for your prosperity by telling everyone. Remember what was given earlier about the power of your words. Once you focus your thoughts and feelings on absolute potential, and the energy starts flowing, your subconscious mind believes you finally mean business about prosperity. You don't want to negate this precious effort by pouring your energy helter-skelter upon all who will listen.
4. *Perfect union between your mind and Macro-Mind produces abundance everlasting and joy beyond expression.* The point of contact is seeking and willingness on your part.

5. *Prosperity cannot be imparted–it must be experienced individually.*
6. *Prosperity doesn't just happen; it's a planned result!* There is nothing "hit or miss" about prosperity. It is as much a planned result as the house in which you live. Without deliberately outlining some prosperity plans, it would be difficult to experience prosperous results on a consistent and permanent basis.

The Law of Persistence

How many good things abound in your life that you never experience or receive? *To be truly prosperous, it is important to receive!* If you don't receive, how can you give freely, either of efficiency or of service in any form?

No man or woman is bound to any undesirable situation. No man or woman is called upon to be resigned to any limiting circumstance. You are not bound; you are not limited. You are free. *You are able to change your life circumstances if you will keep on keeping on!*

Take time every day to quietly experience the living freedom and truth that you can be limited in no manner. The Law of Mental Acceptance explains why some people demonstrate true prosperity and some do not. Those who get results are those who have released the past and have mentally accepted the possibility of new good, total good. Those who hang on to the past and its limitations, reject their own good, and reject the tremendous inner promptings of Macrocosmic Mind trying to give their good to them.

> THERE IS NO SUBSTITUTE FOR THE LAW OF PERSISTENCE!

Whenever you become discouraged; when it seems as if all your best efforts are in vain, remember to hold on to the truth that nothing in the world can take the place of persistence. There is nothing lukewarm or mediocre about persistence. It is bold, daring. It is fearless. Persistence doesn't hesitate at seeming obstacles; it goes after what it wants and keeps plugging away until it gets results.

The average person surrenders too easily to appearances, and throws in the towel, often at the moment when just a little more sincere persistence would press the success button! The word "persist" literally means to "refuse to give up." It is also defined as to "continue firmly, steadily, insistently." So, since you're certainly not an average person, when a time comes into your life when you can't seem to see clearly to definite good ahead, affirm:

> **I continue forward. I am persistent. I am on the way up, not out. I shall keep on keeping on until my good appears.**

Develop the "Can Do" Attitude

Often the Persistence Law of Prosperity is also described as the "Can Do" Attitude. And it works. Look at successful people you know and you will most likely discover that they have cultivated the art or habit of persisting in their chosen goals even in the face of apparent failure. The activities in their life may seem to depict that they have developed an insurance policy against failure. And they have! It may take a little time for them to accomplish a given goal, *but accomplish it they do!* They never allow setbacks to have power in their life. They think big. And often all that is needed is a little more persistence in thinking big, working steadily, and expecting BIG RESULTS in order to bring this manifestation forth in your life.

> PEOPLE WHO CHASE DREAMS ARE THE ONES MOST LIKELY TO CATCH THEM!

The Magic of Increase

So often I hear people ask, "How do I get ahead in life, get a better job or a raise in salary, buy a new car, buy a new house, go on a luxury vacation? How can I have all the money I need to do the things I want to do, when I want to do them?"

There is one sure-fire, workable answer to all these questions. It is simply, LEARN TO USE THE FANTASTIC MACRO-POWER OF YOUR OWN MIND; get in harmony with the Law of Cause and Effect; exercise the Law of Persistence; practice the Law of

Attraction. Each one of these laws works with the same master-precision as do the laws of chemistry, mathematics, and gravitation!

How Nancy L. Invoked the Magic Of Increase in Her Life

Nancy L. came into my office some time ago, the living picture of despondency. Her muffled words were, "I have no job, no money; bills are piling up to the point where I am hounded by collection agencies; my ex-husband has dropped out of sight, and I have a young son to take care of. What am I going to do?"

We talked for a while and I realized that this young woman had a marvelous, sharp mind and tremendous potential in many areas. She was simply experiencing the doldrums and the affairs of life seemed overpowering. As we talked, Nancy realized she had many blessings in her life—marvelous good health, her son was a happy, well-adjusted child; her furniture was paid for.

At my suggestion, she began to take some time each day to pause and give thanks for all the good she was already experiencing. She relaxed her body in an arm chair and entered into a drowsy, semi-sleep state bordering on sleep. This slowed down her conscious mind in order to allow her Superconscious Mind an opportunity to work. Nancy condensed the idea of her preset needs into a powerful magic-making affirmation of increase:

> **The power of Macrocosmic Mind multiplies my good abundantly. I sincerely give thanks for all I now have, and for all that is to come.**

Nancy became aware that whatever she gave her attention to became as a magnet used by her Subconscious Mind and it would be magnified and multiplied a hundred-fold. Then, Nancy selected several sheets of plain yellow paper and cut them into the size of checks which she called her "gold dust checks." She prepared one "gold dust check" for each bill she owed, writing on each "check" the exact amount owed to each creditor, signed the check, and wrote "paid in full" at the bottom of each check. As she did this, Nancy continued to repeat her affirmation for increase.

The idea of using a simple affirmation and a simple action is merely the mechanics of setting into motion a working knowledge of the laws of the mind. When you zero your attention in to one purpose, your mind is prevented from wandering and the power of your thought intensifies, creating an even stronger mental magnet.

Nancy had astounding results. A next door neighbor told her about an exciting new position available in a nearby advertising agency. Armed with her powerful attitude of Macro-Mind thinking, Nancy acquired the position which afforded her an income greater than she had imagined. She became able to meet her financial obligations easily and, after a year on the job, she received an unexpected opportunity to take a much-needed and desired "work-vacation" to the Virgin Islands with her son. At the end of another year, she married her boss's younger brother. When I last saw Nancy, she informed me that all her debts were paid and she is supremely happy with her new life.

The way of the Subconscious Mind is truly miraculous. It has the power to multiply 10-fold, 50-fold, 100-fold your sincere heartfelt desires. This is the marvelous magical law of increase.

The Secret Cause of Indebtedness

Several months ago I was interested in trading cars and shared an interesting conversation with Larry F., the salesman. Our conversation flowed along the lines of how people seem to be using credit privileges at an all-time high, and how the idea of indebtedness related to a rich prosperity consciousness.

Credit is intended to be used *intelligently* to benefit all areas of one's life. it can help you enjoy the comforts and joys of living. It can help you realize a profit in your business. It can help you *establish* a business. It can help you purchase a home, or catapult some dream into reality.

> CREDIT WISELY USED IS A RICH ASSET TO FINANCIAL SUCCESS; BUT CREDIT THAT IS ABUSED IS A STRAIGHT BOULEVARD TO UNNECESSARY INDEBTEDNESS AND FINANCIAL PROBLEMS.

Larry told me about Mr. B., who had came to purchase a truck. Mr. B. came into the showroom, knew exactly the truck he wanted, selected the color he desired from the selection in stock and asked, "Now, how much is the truck?"

Larry answered, "The particular model you have chosen is $7,500.00!"

Mr. B. didn't blink an eye and simply replied, "Fine."

"I was shocked," Larry exclaimed, "when the man didn't try to negotiate the price with me. He merely accepted the figure I quoted him!"

Mr. B. didn't appear to be greatly prosperous—dressed in work clothes. Larry invited him into the sales office and began preparation of the paperwork involved in a sales transaction with a heavy feeling of almost wasting his time. He felt Mr. B. didn't have the financial assets to purchase a truck in the price category he wanted, and he was not trading in any kind of vehicle, so the transaction would be a cash sale. Larry prepared the papers, however, and upon completing the paperwork, turned to Mr. B. and asked, "How do you plan to pay for your truck?"

Mr. B. unceremoniously reached into his back pocket, pulled forth a well-worn wallet, and placed a *certified blank check* in front of Larry with the statement, "You fill in the amount, and just call the bank shown on the face of the check and they will verify my credit!"

Larry did, and learned that Mr. B. was highly regarded as a prime customer of the bank. He had an outstanding credit record, having made a number of credit transactions with the bank and met all his obligations promptly.

Eliminate Fear; Eliminate Indebtedness

If you make a debt with fear filling your heart, then the debt becomes a burden—a heavy weight around your neck. When your thoughts become weighted with this feeling of being burdened, you have thrown up a mental roadblock which hinders the flow of prosperous new ideas coming into your thinking. When the flow of substance is halted by any error thoughts, you become unable to meet your responsibilities and pay your bills. At this point, fear and panic take over.

Let the "Attitude of Gratitude" Prosper You

You can maintain mental control over your financial obligations by facing them with appreciation of the trust expressed in you in the form of credit instead of resenting the bills you have to pay. You can maintain control over your financial obligations by expressing gratitude as you write the checks to pay your bills each month.

When you remain in control of your feelings, instead of allowing yourself to become bound by feelings of indebtedness, you keep the channels open widely for the abundant substance of the universe to flow to you speedily and easily–in both expected and in unexpected ways!

Use the following "Attitude of Gratitude" affirmation:

> **I praise the Universe and give thanks for the immediate and complete payment of all my financial obligations. I attune myself with Macrocosmic Mind and utilize Macro-Mind Power to prosper my financial affairs, making me free, rich, and financially independent.**

Five Ways to Stabilize Your Finances

1. The Universe is filled with "substance," and prosperity is simply substance manifested in your life. Remember that the *true source* of your prosperity is Universal Substance—not a job, a person, a situation—but omnipresent *Universal Substance.*
2. Manage your money wisely and use credit judiciously.
3. Examine and reevaluate your beliefs about money.
4. Express gratitude for the faith which has been shown in you through the extension of credit.
5. Activate the Law of Persistence and hold your thoughts in direct aim toward your targeted goal of debt-free living.

How to Use "Positive Command" to Increase Your Authority Over Life

Shakespeare wrote, "There is a tide in the affairs of men which, taken at the flood, leads on to fortune." I am convinced that he was talking about PCA—Positive Command Attitude! It is through the Law of Positive Command that you achieve dominion over your thoughts, feelings, and actions. By assuming an attitude of authority, you can take control of the good you wish to experience in life.

Let me share a secret with you. *A Positive Command Attitude and verbalization of this attitude regarding the good you wish to obtain is often all that is needed to turn the tide of events to produce the good you desire swiftly and permanently.*

GET DEFINITE ABOUT PROSPERITY,
SO PROSPERITY CAN GET DEFINITE ABOUT YOU.

It's as simple as that! Actually, the Law of Positive Command Attitude is one of the simplest to use. It is the activity of decreeing, speaking the word, asking and receiving!

How Shirley L. Used Positive Command Attitude to Change Her Life

Several years ago, I purchased a home in a new Country Club development. The homes were lovely and comfortable. As I became more acquainted with my next-door neighbor, I realized Shirley used slang expressions constantly and one of her favorite expressions was—"That bugs me!"

I really wasn't surprised when, one morning, she pounded at the door to the sunroom frantically in a state of excitement, frustration, and shock. Shirley had opened a dresser drawer that morning to find hundreds of tiny black specks on her delicate, lacy lingerie! These black specks looked like tiny bugs to Shirley. She called an exterminator, and learned they *were* tiny bugs that had come out of the new lumber in the house and somehow been attracted to that drawer! How these unwelcome creatures of nature got into her dresser drawer remains a mystery, but Shirley is one lady who will never again say, "That bugs me!"

This experience of Shirley's opened the door for us to have some fantastic conversations about the tremendous power of maintaining a *Positive Command Attitude!*

You Make Your World with Your Words

You are constantly using the *Positive Command Attitude* because you are constantly using words; although your words may often produce the wrong kinds of decrees!

Another acquaintance of mine, often remarked, "I can't stand that!" as she curled her lips and wrinkled her nose in disdain for whatever was the momentary target. She uttered this phrase several times a day for several months until, one morning, as Beth was leaving her home for work, she took a disastrous tumble, breaking her leg severely in three places! She lugged around a heavy cast encasing her leg from toe to thigh for almost six months. Fortunately, she was alert and aware enough to realize that for months she had been proclaiming just what happened in her life.

Create a Wonder-Working Vacuum

It is often said that nature abhors a vacuum. And this statement is absolutely, positively true! The *Vacuum Law of Prosperity* is powerful, but it sometimes requires a bold, daring *faith* to set it into operation! A sense of great adventure and high expectations is also helpful. So often I've seen folks who were sincerely and honestly trying to become more prosperous and who were putting all the tools into action, yet nothing happened. Why? Because they had usually forgotten to use the *Vacuum Law of Prosperity.*

Question: *What is the Vacuum Law of Prosperity?*

Answer: *It's very simple. Get rid of the junk in your life that you don't want in order to make room for that good which you do desire!*

If there is old furniture cluttering your garage or basement, get rid of it. If ancient, unused clothes fill your closets, give them away. If you have acquaintances or "friends" who no longer seem congenial, release them from your life. *Start now to move the tangibles and the intangibles from your life which are no longer useful and meaningful to you.* The results you will experience, and the uplift you will feel will be surprising. And remember—*it is sometimes difficult to know exactly what you do want until you clear the way by eliminating what you don't want!*

How the Vacuum Law of Prosperity Worked for Me

When I left Seminary School after three years of study and training, I didn't want to pay the heavy moving expenses of transporting furniture across the country. Besides, my furniture, after two children, two dogs, and a cat, and several major moves, looked as if it had come over on the Mayflower and couldn't survive another move! I decided to "practice what I preached" and put the Vacuum Law of Prosperity to work. Fearlessly, I gave away the majority of pieces of furniture to a young couple who had just been married six months and were trying to establish a home. They were thrilled! My "not-so-goods" became their prized possessions for the time being, and I had bare spaces to stare at in my home.

But I was excited! The moving van came and loaded my china, crystal, linens, etc., and headed east. I purchased a nice townhouse apartment in my new location. It had a yummy color scheme and unlimited possibilities. My old furniture would have looked like the wreck of the Hesperus in this bright, new place. I lovingly and happily arranged the china, crystal, linens, clothes, and plants, and in the bare places visualized just the items I wanted. There was vast opportunity for visualization, for I had brought the stereo equipment, a lovely chest, a cherished desk and chair, and a bookcase as my only furniture!

For a few weeks, nothing seemed to happen, but I could *feel* the excitement growing. Then, a large furniture store had a tremendous clearance sale on their quality furniture items, and I had a bonanza. A long-time friend was moving, and gave me a gorgeous antique credenza which I had long admired in her home! People from my congregation learned of my love for plants and my townhouse looks like a tropical garden. I even have a fantastic Fica tree in my living room! Within *four months*, my new townhouse looked like the center foldout of a posh interior decorating magazine and I had spent a nominal amount of money!

There is only one real power you can use—Macro-Mind Power—*and it loves to be used.* You cannot manipulate it, but you can sure use it for all kinds of fantastic good.

Power Pointers for Using Positive Command Attitudes

1. The spoken word moves on the invisible planes; forms Macro-Mind *Substance* into definite results; and gives the manifestation birth in the physical, visible world.
2. "What you utter, becomes outer!"
3. General words do not produce specific results. Color your words vividly with thought, feeling, and visualization.
4. Audible and inaudible words are equally important and effective!

5. Spoken words quickly help turn the tide of defeat. Persistence pays!
6. Open your mind and consciousness to the divine idea of prosperity.
7. Where your attention abides, there your *whole consciousness* lives. *Use your attention constructively.*
8. Enlarge your capacity to receive by creating a Prosperity Vacuum.
9. Give generously and with joy and with no tought of receiving, and your good will come! *Prosperity is unending. As you empty your cup, the Universe REFILLS IT!*
10. Realize . . . understand . . . know there is no such thing as lack.

MACRO-MIND "PROSPERITY" MOTIVATORS

1. If you truly want to be prosperous, you can be!
2. Build a Prosperity Atmosphere around you. Your thoughts, feelings, and words are seeds. Sow a good crop of abundance by choosing your seeds with care!
3. Your financial income cannot be limited. The power of Macro-Mind, and the unlimited rich substance of the Universe flows to you now, freeing you from all financial limitation.
4. Let your poised manner be one of quiet good and prosperity and you will attract prosperous persons and activities.
5. Life is a series of transformations and manifestations of energy. So is prosperity!
6. Work is a joyful and harmonious part of you, and the Universe is a generous paymaster!
7. Watch your words! They are more powerful than you may realize. Utilize the Positive Command Attitude to work for you, not against you.
8. Refuse to criticize or condemn anyone or anything if you desire to become and remain debt-free. Remember that an "Attitude of Gratitude" prospers you.
9. Start where you are. Use what is at hand right now, and "Keep On Keeping On"!

4

How Macro-Mind Power Can Create Riches and Abundance for You

You Can Have Everything!

The sales representatives of a successful business firm I know are as carefully selected as the sales promotion ideas the firm projects for future growth. The executives of this firm know that salesmen who are honest, happy, and constructive, and who believe in the products they sell, *secure large and very profitable orders.*

It is a realized fact that *good salesmen produce good results!* These same executives also know that salesmen who are careless in their manner, negative in their speech, and who have no faith in the products they sell, not only fail to bring in meaningful orders, but they are a financial drain on the firm's treasury. *These wise executives keep a close watch on their sales representatives and weed out all the ones who are unproductive!*

Who are you but a *top executive!* What are your thoughts but *salesmen of your mind!* Poor executives are careless in their selection of thought agents. They permit these thought agents to wander into bypaths, to become entangled with discouragements, troubles, and disease. Poor executives will say, "I need more money. I shall ask for a raise in salary, but then, of course, I shall not get it. That's just my luck—to be turned down!"

Such a person has sent out salesmen who have no confidence in what they represent. Instead of going in the right direction, they stray off into negative paths, and nothing good or desirable is accomplished. Of course, these thought agents return empty-handed to the executive. When you send good words into the universal ethers, they bring back good results, but they will not bring the maximum of good unless positive thought vibrations go with them.

Good words and negative thoughts, or negative words and good thoughts are a house divided against itself *and it must come crashing down!* Until you reach unity in thought and speech, until your mental house is no longer divided against itself, until your thoughts and your words are so unified in perfection that they go hand in hand after whatever the executive may desire, results will be mediocre.

You attain your greatest success and highest manifestation of good when your constructive thoughts and constructive words are backed by faith in yourself, in your fellow man, and above all, in the wonder-working power of Macrocosmic Mind.

> WHEN YOU BECOME AWARE OF THE COLOSSAL MACRO-POWER THAT IS WITHIN YOU AND *DARE TO USE IT*, YOU CAN HAVE EVERYTHING!

As long as you have been in embodiment on this earth, *you have used this Macro-Power to some degree.* Now, you can consciously take charge of your life and deliberately use this marvelous power to achieve success and for experiencing greater happiness in all areas of your life.

This success power is released through your emotional reactions toward life and through your mental attitudes. You are now, and will become what you think and feel. Think and feel success and you become success. Think and feel poverty-stricken or lack and you become a "loser" in life.

How to Create New Opportunities

Have you ever heard the old saying, "When an old door closes, a new and better one opens"? It's true. *Believe it!* In my own life I've had many doors seemingly slammed in my face, almost bruising my nose, yet, even as I turned away in disappointment, I spotted a new, more meaningful opportunity headed my way! Whenever any old activity comes to an end, you have the productive power of Macrocosmic Mind within you to create a new opportunity that will offer new occurrences to express your talents and ability more fully.

Question: *How can I bring this activity about?*
Answer: *Use new Opportunity Door Openers!*

Six Amazingly Effective Opportunity Door Openers You Can Use

1. Think of the job position or activity you really desire to do.
2. Determine that you will involve yourself in this work or activity, even if it means "starting at the bottom."
3. Refuse to settle for less than one-hundred percent performance in your chosen field.
4. Determine that you will be the greatest person ever to be engaged in your chosen field of work. Whatever it is that you decide to do, determine that you will be the best. *This is simply having a high vision of yourself—a mental vision that will lead to fame and fortune.*
5. Act as if you *already are* the best person in the work you desire. This action has nothing to do with personal ego, it is simply the sincere desire and determination on your part *to be that which you are meant to be!*
6. Use the power of your MACRO-VISION, combined with positive belief as you've never used it before to inwardly KNOW that you already are what you desire to be. If the desire wasn't true and obtainable, *you wouldn't have it in the first place!* Know that this is true and continue to know it is true until the truth becomes a manifestation in your life!

How to Make the Right Decision When Opportunities Arrive

Often I've found that by placing myself totally in tune with my desires through monitoring my thoughts, feelings, and actions, not one, but *several* similar opportunities will come. Then it becomes necessary to make a decision regarding which of the available opportunities is the right one.

Here is the fail-proof method I use for arriving at a right decision. Weigh both the good points and the "not-so-good" points in each opportunity realistically. Don't be blinded by over-eager enthusiasm, but set aside your emotional feelings and look at each opportunity clearly.

Get a sheet of paper for each opportunity and at the top of each sheet, write the details of the opportunity. Under this description, on the left side of your sheet of paper, write "FAVORABLE AS-

PECTS," and on the right side of the sheet of paper, write "UNFAVORABLE ASPECTS."

Now, analyze the opportunity. List everything pertaining to that opportunity that you can think of under the proper heading. After you've done this for each opportunity, then ask yourself the following questions in an overview of the total opportunities presented.

1. Which opportunity offers the greatest avenue for progress?
2. Which opportunity offers me *complete freedom* to express my talents and ability in the *most effective* manner?
3. Which opportunity offers the greatest working conditions?
4. Which opportunity offers me greater financial income?
5. Which opportunity do I feel most comfortable with regarding the people involved?
6. Which opportunity intuitively "feels" right for me?

Now, look at your columns marked "FAVORABLE ASPECTS" and "UNFAVORABLE ASPECTS." You will be able to perceive which of the opportunities available offers the most benefits and is the right choice for you. This same method can be used in reaching a right decision about any matter.

How Anne B. Helped Her Husband Create a Fabulous New Job Opportunity

I lived next door to Anne B. and her husband Leonard for three years. Anne and I shared many hours of friendship and discussion about the dynamic laws of MACRO-MIND POWER. She was skeptical in the beginning, and then settled on the attitude of "What the heck; what have I got to lose?"

Leonard worked for a large manufacturing corporation whose offices and plants were scattered throughout the world. Anne and Leonard owned a comfortable middle-class home and lived a comfortable middle-class way of life. They enjoyed travel, and inasmuch as Leonard's company was an international one, there was no reason why the two of them couldn't participate in exciting travel experiences.

Anne talked with Leonard. His enthusiasm was lukewarm, but Anne decided that she would make something happen. And she did! Anne began working with Prosperity Door Openers, holding a powerful vision of her husband receiving a nice promotion and increased responsibilities in his work, resulting in a boost in salary. She also held the Macro-Vision of Leonard making frequent trips for his company in the United States and abroad.

Anne followed her Macro-Visualization by *taking an action step.* She began looking at fashionable sports clothes suitable for travel, and picked up several colorful brochures from the local travel agency of exotic places they wanted to visit.

Within six months, Leonard received a promotion, making him head of his department and increasing his salary by $300 per month! Part of the job's responsibilities included travel, and the company policy stated that when one of their executives traveled abroad for more than a month, the spouse could go along!

Within a year, Leonard was sent to Switzerland to help establish a new nuclear power plant for the company. Anne was elated! For seven months she and Leonard lived in Switzerland and had a super-fantastic experience! Anne was convinced. As she continued to invoke the success attitude of Opportunity Door Openers, Leonard inherited a nice sum of money from his father's estate which enabled them to purchase some lake property twenty miles from their home. Anne's only remark to me about a year later was a toss of her head and a hearty, "*I'm convinced! This stuff really works!*"

How to Choose Things That Will Do You the Most Good!

If you are the owner of a business and become dissatisfied with your work accommodations because they no longer are sufficient to meet your needs, you know that you can find larger, more effective quarters in another location. The same analogy holds true if you are dissatisfied with circumstances and conditions in your life. The first step is making up your mind that you are going to have greater success and move out of your present condition and into new and greater opportunities. *Right now is the time to take out your personal shiny new lease on life!* Goethe said,

> The impossible is often still possible to those who are prudent and circumspect.

Decide not only to *want* greater abundance, greater meaning in your life, but dare to *reach out* for it and *claim* your good! As long as timidity deceives you into believing that something is impossible, it will remain just that—impossible. But if you refuse to limit yourself, you are able to cross the barriers that hold back so many others. You can be bold—and this action in itself will give you greater opportunities to break through into outstanding achievements.

Unshakable faith and the daring courage to do what others term "impossible" makes a person a leader. The leader sees what is necessary and knows that a new day always follows the dark of the night. The man of vision sees that it is only in appearances that something is "impossible." His positive attitude gives him that inner assurance and sustenance which makes him stronger than any circumstance. And the more he expects and demands of himself in performance and achievement, the greater are the things he accomplishes. *This is the truth about you.* YOU ARE INFINITELY GREATER THAN YOU THINK!

Check yourself out . . . your aspirations, your hopes, your faith in your abilities. Who knows what great possibilities of accomplishments are in store for you!

Why You Don't Have to Be Poor!

Prosperity is your spiritual right! And true prosperity includes not just having enough money to meet your needs, but having *abundant* money to meet your requirements and to do the things which you wish to do in total peace and harmony.

The Universe is created lavishly and on a grand scale. If you *really* want something to manifest in your life, you must start somewhere. By defining your needs, you are giving Macrocosmic Mind an opportunity to focus on you and your needs and start working to bring your desires into manifestation.

Question: *Why do you want more money in your life?*

Answer: *Because money is the medium through which you can enjoy a higher standard of living.* But this isn't the only reason. *The primary reason is that your mind has fantastic power to produce wealth,*

> *and when you desire to receive wealth in the form of money and believe it will come, the power of Macrocosmic Mind will cause money to be drawn to you.* You are setting into action a MACRO-MENTAL MONEY MAGNET!

Why Some People Are Poor

Most people who experience being poor and not having sufficient money do so because they believe in LACK instead of ABUNDANCE. Folks who believe in this manner are failing to realize that *the true source of all wealth is within them,* and this nonrealization is a block keeping the prosperity flow from reaching them.

Charles Fillmore said this about money:

> Watch your thoughts when you are handling your money, because your money is attached through your mind to the one Source of all substance and all money.
>
> *Keep a True Lent,* p. 102, Unity Books.

Substance is Omnipresent, Living Energy. It is the "etheric" form from which everything is formed. Your every thought and feeling and word—from the smallest to the greatest—acts upon this substance.

The Macro-Money Magnet Technique

As you are preparing for bed each evening, think about your monetary needs. Visualize this amount of money in your Macro-Mirror exercise, painting a vivid mental picture. Then, take the following affirmative steps.

1. I need $___________ right now to pay off all old bills, leaving me debt-free.
2. I need $___________ in monthly income to adequately meet all my needs.
3. I desire $___________ in extra money to be able to persue a specific desire. (This could be a special vacation, new clothes, new furniture, whatever would bring you comfort, joy, and satisfaction.)

4. Affirm: **I know the fulfillment of this need and desire exists in the cosmic universe.**
5. Affirm: **I know the fulfillment of this need and desire can come through both known and unknown channels.**
6. Affirm: **Complete fulfillment is moving toward me NOW and I joyfully accept my good!**
7. I take the needed steps in preparation for my rich fulfillment by
   (a) Giving freely and joyfully to others, and
   (b) By doing everything I know to prepare to receive my good.
8. I joyfully give thanks for abundant prosperity NOW.

Now, speak positively to your subconscious mind using the Positive Command Attitude. Say, "*Subconscious Mind, I have presented you with a mental picture of the money amount I need and desire. I desire to receive $—————— within* (name the specified time, one week, month, year.") and be realistic! "*I now command you to go to work and deliver the required sum of money to me!*"

Then, relax and go to sleep knowing that you have set the wheels in motion and your wish will become a reality. Continue to work with this Money Magnet Technique for a period of six months and you will attract more money than you can imagine. Remember what was given earlier about persistence! Six months may seem like a long time, but how does it stack up against the rest of your life? Isn't it worth while to give a few minutes for a period of time in your life to become rich, prosperous, and happy?

How A 72-Year-Old Man Used The MACRO-MONEY MAGNET to Obtain a Permanent Job at a Salary of $6,000!

Leo F. was feeling about as low as the fallen rose petals in his garden. His small farm at the edge of town barely afforded food and shelter, and his Social Security allotment was scantily providing the break-even point. Leo was strong and healthy, despite his years, and wanted a better legacy from life.

Leo decided to take action, and *one of the greatest of all success attitudes is the willingness to do something positive to help bring about your desires!* Leo had attended some "positive thinking" classes and he vaguely remembered something in his notes about a Money Magnet Technique. He rummaged through his desk and found the desired notes. As he prepared for bed that night, Leo thought about his monetary needs. He thought about his essential needs; and he thought about how nice it would be to have some "extra" money. He could visit his granddaughter in Colorado; he could subscribe to a couple of magazines he liked; and his mind enumerated several other things he wanted to do. Immediately the figure of $6,000 popped into his mind and Leo said, "O.K., that's what I'll use!"

About a month later, a friend came by to see Leo and to purchase some cuttings from his rose bushes. Leo was a "green thumb" gardner and produced the loveliest roses in the county. As Leo and his friend ambled through the garden, it was easy to see the love and attention with which Leo tended his flowers. The friend recognized this tender caring immediately and said, "Leo, how would you like a job tending a rose garden for a large organization?"

Leo's blue eyes sparkled. "Yeah! You think they'd hire me?"

"Well, it certainly won't hurt to ask!"

Leo called the organization, went to their office for an interview, fell in love with the magnificent large rose garden landscaped around beautiful fountains, and was hired for the position!

Leo is now a "permanent fixture" on the grounds of this organization, and everyone loves him as much as he enjoys and loves his work!

A Universal Formula for Prosperity

A $12,000 department head was summoned to the president's office. He felt uneasy, but reassured himself that everything must be all right. Profits had escalated about ten percent during the year he had been running the department. Arming himself with his latest Profit and Loss Statement, he headed "upstairs."

The president said, "Jim, I see you have some good stuff in you, but your department showed a profit of only $100,000 this year."

"Yes, Mr. Wells, but that's ten percent over last year."

Mr. Wells paused, smiled. Then came the haymaker: "In the

next two years I want to see your department show a profit of one million dollars."

Jim thought the president was joking. After all . . . a ten-times increase! But the president was not joking. What's more, he told Jim he could keep his present staff but he could not increase it! When Jim showed a million dollars in profits, his salary would be jumped to $25,000 and he'd be in line for more!

The president saw Jim's shock, heard his slightly dazed, "I'll try." Yet by the time Jim returned to his office, he was moving in a new world. He sat down and made lists of every process, every sales method he used. Soon he saw ways to save on manufacturing costs. His product was books, and he realized he'd never tried to sell books a thousand at a time to big corporations. And why not bring out a $300 Culture Library? And what about the market for art prints, using the thousands of names of customers he already had in his files? And what about . . ." Jim's mind raced.

He'd never had to think ten times bigger. Now he did, and he communicated the excitement of his feeling to his entire staff. In two years his profits were $1,180,284, and he said that was peanuts!

You, too, can use the *Ten-Times Technique.* This technique is truly one of the greatest of all psychological miracles. When you set your sights on king-sized goals, your subconscious mind starts automatically seeking ways to supply whatever is needed to reach these goals. You can use this *Ten-Times Technique* to skyrocket your present income . . . to become the most proficient employee in your company . . . to become the greatest secretary in the company . . . to become a fabulous homemaker . . . to accomplish anything you want, without limit!

Recognize that there is an abundant supply of Macro-Mind Power ready to go to work for you. The known sources of your good may be numerous, but the unknown sources are *infinite!* Open your mind to channels of yet unknown good, as well as known channels of good.

Fulfillment exists in time and space. There is an abundant supply of money, energy, people, work, homes, jobs, love, good health. Take the necessary steps in preparation for receiving your "Ten-Times" good!

- Decide to be the most valuable person in the field of your present work.

- Give more efficiently and effectively of your time and service.
- Put greater enthusiasm into what you are presently doing—whether work or play!
- Think up new ideas that will benefit your present position.
- Visualize yourself receiving a big promotion with a large salary increase.

How to Make Your Master Demonstration

Question: *What is a Master Demonstration?*
Answer: *A Master Demonstration is a giant dream come true, a gigantic result happening in your life; it is your greatest prayer answered magnificently!*

A Master Demonstration consists not only of the "big event," but always includes many smaller beneficial results as extra "side effects."

We have talked about exercising your ability to give. It is time now to discuss your amazing ability to receive! You cannot be a successful *giver* if you aren't a gracious *receiver!* Giving and receiving are the two ends of the Law of Cause and Effect. You simply can't have one without the other. *Giving is only half of the success law!* And if you are unable to receive, you simply "gum up the works" and deflect your good. It is vitally important to be a good receiver, for this activity opens fantastic avenues for abundant riches.

All the giving you've already done through the years has been like investing money in a Cosmic Savings Account. Your giving has been invested, accumulated cosmic interest, and now is ready to return to you with that interest! Perhaps your invested good hasn't yet returned to you because you didn't *expect to receive*, and haven't opened your mind to the idea of receiving your accumulated good in manifested tangible ways.

How to Use Macro-Emotive Reminders To Help You Make Your Master Demonstration

Whatever your age, whatever your dreams, whatever you want from life, you can find tremendously increased results of success and happiness by helping yourself with Macro-Emotive Reminders. You're never too old, and it's never too late to make your Master Demonstration. All your life you've been reminding yourself that you want to be successful, you want to be richer, you want to be happier, you want to look more radiant, you want to draw more exciting people to you. Now, you can use this mighty prosperity technique to obtain exactly what you wish, to experience exactly the results you desire. Get going now, and let these Macro-Emotive Reminders expand your bank account—cosmically and materially!

MACRO-EMOTIVE REMINDERS

- *I determine to maintain my zest for living. I never really lost it, but merely sidetracked it for a while!*
- *A person is as old as he or she feels! I feel young, vitally alive, zestful, rich, energetic, and happy!*
- *My goal is a richer, fuller, more prosperous life. This dream is mine to claim now. I know it, and I show it!*
- *I determine to use my life experiences to build a truly meaningful and fantastic life. I profit from all experience-gained knowledge!*
- *I continue to learn, thereby, constantly expanding my own consciousness to include increasing amounts of life's abundance.*
- *I determine to begin each day with the enthusiastic feeling that it's great to be alive. I face each new day as a great adventure. I* expect *good happenings, and I* experience *great events!*
- *I determine to expand my world beyond my present everyday surroundings and stimulate myself with interesting things to do and the company of interesting people!*
- *I determine to be open and receptive and lovingly allow myself to receive graciously!*
- *I determine to be patient, kind, tolerant, and understanding in my relationships with others. I hereby declare that from this moment forward, my normal condition is one of peace, serenity, and happiness!*
- *I determine to "tune in" to MACRO-ENERGY, relaxing as I work with the realization that I have sufficient energy to accomplish all the requirements of my day—and some to spare!*

- *I know that it is divinely right for me to be rich! I now cast aside all ideas of limitations and look for ways I can use the dynamic laws of prosperity in my life!*

Make a Success Covenant Between Yourself and Macro-Mind Power

A "covenant" is a binding agreement, usually made between two people, to do a special thing in order to achieve definite and desired results. Right now, you can take what could be the most important step of your life and decide to make a success covenant between yourself and the "sure-fire" power of Macrocosmic Mind! You don't have to wait until things start to "look up" in your life to begin. Regardless of where you are on the ladder of success, you can make a definite prosperity covenant with Macro-Mind Power.

Question: *What is a covenant again?*
Answer: *A covenant is a two-part agreement, requiring specific action on the part of both parties.*

Your covenant with Macro-Mind Power will look like this:

A. A statement of what you wish Macro-Mind Power to help you achieve, and

B. A statement of what you will do for Macro-Mind Power.

Now, most covenants are made for a specific period of time, so establish a definite period of time in your mind regarding your covenant—a month, two months, six months, or whatever time you feel is meaningful, important, and realistic.

Place your covenant in a safe place where you will be able to reread it at will, yet it will be safe from inquisitive eyes of others.

Begin immediately to start upholding your part of the covenant.

At regular intervals, check your written covenant to review actions you may need to take and to observe what results have transpired. Mark the things off from your covenant list where results have been obtained and remember to express gratitude to the Universe and to Macrocosmic Mind for helping bring about these results.

When the time span of your first covenant period expires, make a new covenant for new dreams and desires in your life for a new stipulated period. Your success will be amazing.

Just to help get you going, I'll share with you a tremendously successful covenant I prepared.

MY SUCCESS COVENANT
March 20, 19—

Part One: (My commitment)

1. I desire $3,000 in clear, free cash to pay all school indebtedness, within four months.
2. I desire a constant, debt-free monthly income NOW, beginning at $1,000 per month, plus travel expenses.
3. I desire to write many best-selling books over the coming years.
4. I am grateful ALWAYS!

Part Two: (My commitment to Macro-Mind)

1. I will joyfully pay my school indebtedness, and live the gratitude I feel in my soul so others may be bathed in my light.
2. I will use this income wisely, living in accordance with my goals and desires, and sharing with others in whatever ways I can be helpful.
3. I will seek to make each manuscript for each book meaningful and an important guideline for those who read these books to find greater expression of themselves through helping themselves with Cosmic Powers.
4. I am grateful ALWAYS!

How Jane B. Attracted the Right Buyer for Her House

After I gave a metaphysical lecture at a college campus, a young woman from the faculty approached me and said, "I really want to sell my house so I can purchase another one. However, I've been unable to sell it. What can I do to attract the right buyer for my house?"

I asked her if she *really believed* she could attract a buyer for her house who was as eager to buy it as she was to sell it.

Jane thought about this for a moment and then nodded affirmatively. Then, I gave her the Success Covenant which I have just given you and suggested that she prepare her personal Success Covenant and set a time-target of thirty days. Here's what happened.

Jane decided to use the Success Covenant. She prepared her covenant, listing all the ways she wished Macro-Mind Power to assist her. Next, she listed all the ways she could assist Macro-Mind Power in helping attract the right buyer.

A week later, Jane was invited to a dinner party where she met a new real estate broker in town who was in the process of establishing a sales office. This broker was eager to attract business to his new office and Jane mentioned she had a lovely home for sale which she had been trying to sell herself. The broker was interested and arranged an appointment with Jane for the next day to see her property. He was impressed with the architectural characteristics and gracious charm of her home and contracted with Jane to list the property exclusively for thirty days!

One week later, the broker telephoned, requesting an appointment to show the house. His client was impressed with Jane's lovely home and within three days made arrangements to purchase it! The contracts were signed and the deal was closed within a month!

Jane was estatic! The client found a lovely home, the real estate broker made a nice commission, and Jane was able to purchase the new property she desired.

What transpired in this instance? *Jane was willing to accept the truth that Macro-Mind Power would work with her in achieving her desires. She prepared the Success Covenant and then faithfully followed through on her part of the covenant.* This resulted in setting into motion the powerful Law of Cause and Effect, and the Law of Attraction, and the right person was attracted to her property and a sale was consummated!

Success Formulas for Increasing Your Prosperity

1. Substance plus Thoughts equals Manifestation!
2. Thinking plus Feeling equals Demonstration!
3. Quantity plus Quality plus Mental Attitude equals Compensation!

4. Asking plus Expecting equals Getting!
5. Prosperity Consciousness plus Constructive Action equals Opulence!
6. Praise plus Gratitude equals Manifested Good!
7. Blessing minus Doubt equals Prosperity!

MACRO-MIND "RICHES AND ABUNDANCE" MOTIVATORS!

1. Opportunity begins in your mind, in your magnificent imagination. This is why people who have terrific imagination experience abundant opportunities.
2. Promise yourself to continually look at the sunny side of everything, letting your optimism be a constant companion that helps make your dreams come true.
3. Think only the best: work for the best: expect the best: accept only the best: be the best!
4. Be too big for worry, too noble for anger, too strong for fear, too persistent for defeat, too happy for disharmony!
5. Adopt a new attitude of loving willingness toward all things.
6. The Light of Macrocosmic Mind shines within you, dispelling the darkness of ignorance and revealing the light of opportunity.
7. You are the ever-renewing, ever-unfolding, ever-prosperous, unique expression of the magnificent and incorruptible Universe. Act like it!
8. Have an ideal and live up to it!
9. When you rule your mind, you rule your world!
10. Every moment is a right moment when you are attuned with Macrocosmic Mind.
11. You are a living improvement!
12. The only thing that can ever be wrong with you is the fact that you *think* there is something wrong with you!

5

How Macro-Mind Power Can Help You Create A Cosmic Treasure Map!

You Have Special Powers!

Regardless of who you are—or where you may reside—you are always a dynamo of Macro-Power within. When you learn to use this magnificent power, it provides you with a new, exciting and wonderful life.

Macro-Power not only works, *it's natural and normal*—not supernatural as some people think. In short, you don't have to work in dimly lighted rooms, go into trances, or be exotically different. Most people have little understanding of their own ability to use Macro-Power. But many a doubter becomes a devotee once he's experimented with the success of this marvelous force! The beautiful aspect of it is, *the more you use it, the easier and better it gets!*

Nothing is impossible if you really want to accomplish it! In this Aquarian age of space travel, and interplanetary equipment like space modules Pioneer 10 and Mariner 10, the deeper powers of your mind, which have been virtually dormant in earlier eras, are now blooming profusely.

These deeper powers of your mind are described by scientists and parapsychologists as Telepathy, Clairvoyance and Precognition, and Extrasensory Perception. Let's take a closer look at these special powers from a point of view of understanding how each one can increase your prosperity.

Prosperity is an absolutely fascinating commodity. It means different things to different people. To one, prosperity means a fine home, a new car every year, dues paid at a posh country club. To another, prosperity may mean a new bungalow on five wooded acres. Radiant good health spells prosperity to some, while others look at it as security in love, the right mate. Still others see prosperity as power they can wield in their life. Couldn't it mean a little of each . . . and more, to you? I hope so.

What does it take to attract *total* prosperity?

Telepathy—And How the Ancients Used It

Telepathy is defined as a direct mind-to-mind communication between two or more persons. Telepathy is the awareness of the mental activities of others, an awareness that is not transmitted by sight, hearing, touch, or any of the other known senses.

From New York to San Francisco,
From Earth to Mars,

MIND HAS NO LIMITATION IN TIME AND SPACE!

There is nothing spectacular about telepathy. It is as natural a universal law as the Law of Gravity. The native Hawaiians practiced telepathy for centuries, long before the white man appeared on the scene to "civilize" the natives. In Tahiti, friends and relatives used telepathy to communicate with each other. In Africa, news of political decisions has been known to be received telepathically, sometimes days before it was officially announced. In the Far East, Holy Men and great masters practiced telepathy as a common mental exercise for centuries. In our present time, men such as Dr. Al Manning in California, Dr. J. B. Rhine of North Carolina, and others have worked diligently to make telepathy scientifically plausible.

Development of your telepathic power helps you in *all* areas. It minimizes needless conversations, telephone calls, letters, fatiguing activities that are time consuming and energy-draining. Development of this marvelous power increases your sense of poise and serenity, and aids in accomplishing essential tasks more easily.

How to Develop Telepathy in Yourself

If you desire to develop this tremendous ability within yourself, it is important to eliminate all stray thoughts and feelings of your own, while either sending or receiving a telepathic message. Your mind operates like a television set. If the set isn't properly and finely tuned, the picture is blurred and interference from a nearby or overlapping channel can cause difficulty. This creates distortion, and you may have to guess at what you are receiving. In the case of telepathy, your interference comes from conflicting thoughts and feelings in your own mind.

If you wish to send a message, sit quietly, eyes closed, holding the image in your consciousness of the person you wish to contact. Speak to him or her quietly, softly, so you hear your own voice, while imagining that he or she is present with you. State your message. Hold a conscious image of the person another minute, then release the entire action.

You can send a loving message to your boss of how efficiently you do your job. You can send a loving message of sincerity to someone you desire to get to know better. You can send a healing message of love to someone with whom you are in disagreement.

In receiving a telepathic message, there is a very definite *feeling* that comes. So, the next time you get a feeling "out of the blue" *stop everything and pay attention to it!* One message I received in this manner was a definite feeling I should call a dear friend. I called. The friend was barely able to answer the telephone, he was so sick. Immediately I went to his home and took him to the hospital. What would have happened if I had not *listened* to the *inner* prompting?

How to Use Your Clairvoyant and Precognitive Ability to Increase Your Prosperity

Clairvoyance means to see and feel events, objects, and conditions at a distance, either past or present. It is a special power for prosperity. *It is an awareness of external facts or events without having such knowledge transmitted to you by any one of the five senses.*

Scientists sometimes describe one phase of clairvoyance as "*Precognitive,*" *which means to know about a future event before it occurs, either through a dream, a vision, or a feeling.*

An important key in the development of Clairvoyance is in *knowing* that you want to *heighten your awareness* of external facts and events through the help of Macrocosmic Mind.

I once knew a man who developed his clairvoyant or precognitive abilities along such positive lines that he instinctively "knew" exactly the right sales program to implement and the right time to set it into motion. His aim was to produce a quality product, sell it at a reasonable profit, and provide good service for his product when needed. His company grew in gigantic leaps, going from a mere one-half million dollars in annual sales to fifteen million dollars in annual sales within seven years!

Another example is a woman I know who used her clairvoyant or precognitive abilities along negative lines, creating sad conditions of unbalance and destruction for herself. As a result, her health failed, her emotions were shattered, her husband and children left her, and the return trip to a semblance of normal living was long and difficult. Her situation simply bore out the universal law that *like always attracts like in the realm of mind.*

How Laura T.'s Precognitive Ability Saved Her Life

On a beautiful Saturday morning in April, Laura T. was experiencing a relaxing drive in the Allegheny mountains of West Virginia and simply absorbing all the beauty about her. Rhododendrons covered the mountainsides in a fantasy of pink, white, red, and purple. New growth was at the mint-green stage of bursting forth on the trees, and thick emerald grass covered the gentle slopes like a soft carpet.

A speed limit sign slid into view around a winding curve, stating "35 miles per hour-maximum safe speed." Well, that was rather slow, but the morning was too beautiful to hurry through, and Laura was enjoying the wonderous attunement she felt with the world.

Suddenly, a chill streaked down her spine and she recalled the vivid details of a dream she had experienced several nights previously. In her dream loomed a speed limit sign very similar to the one she had just passed, and in the dream, about a mile beyond the sign, a terrible accident had occurred.

Suddenly, with the clarity of a trumpet blast, a voice inside her being called, "Slow down!" She glanced at her speedometer on the car, and it read "35 miles per hour." Immediately her human reasoning said, "But you're really crawling at a snail's pace; why should you slow down more?" Again, appeared the images of the dream and with even more powerful emphasis the inner voice screamed, "Slow down!"

Instinctively Laura obeyed.

Rolling over and around the mountains at 25 miles per hour seemed ridiculous! And Laura could see in her rear view mirror that the driver of another car which had come up behind her was impatient to pass, but the winding mountain road didn't permit him to do so. Yet, she knew instinctively that it was important to obey that inner voice and maintain her speed.

Suddenly she crested the mountaintop, and there traveling toward her at rapid speed in her lane of traffic was a large tractor-trailer truck, passing three cars! There was no time to think, only to act. She remembered hearing the words, "Oh, God, help us!" explode from her lips as she jammed the brakes on the car and clutched the steering wheel.

On her right was a stone embankment, and on her left was a drop of about seventy-five feet down the mountainside. It looked like disaster, but after what seemed like minutes, all the vehicles came to a screeching halt. Her car had slid into the V-shape made when the truck veered into the embankment, and the other cars ran off the road as far as they could without going over the edge of the cliff. Somehow the man behind her had managed to stop without colliding. Yet, had Laura not listened to the voice speaking to her from within and slowed down, a serious accident could have occurred. How much more specific could precognition have been than to tell her to slow down!

How to Use Your Power Of Extra-Sensory Perception

First, I'd like to toss out the word "extra" and replace it with "natural." What seems to be "extra" or supernatural ability of the mind is merely an extension of the natural ability you possess. ESP is a blending of Telepathy, where you become aware of the thoughts of other people, and of Clairvoyance and Precognition, where you become aware of events or facts that are taking place.

Can you remember times when you sensed that something wonderful was going to happen, yet you had no idea of what it would be? Have you also experienced a feeling of foreboding that something unpleasant was near, which caused you to become uncertain or unsure?

A knock came at my door one morning as I was preparing breakfast. Opening the door, I came face to face with a member of my congregation who looked as if the cat had trapped him the night before.

I clasped Paul by the hand and pulled him into the foyer and invited him to have a cup of coffee. As we sat drinking the coffee, he described a dream he had experienced the night before, and his difficulty of shaking a terrible feeling of "something being very wrong." In his dream, the primal figure was a beloved sister. I suggested he call his sister to set his mind at rest that everything was in order.

Paul left for his office. Three hours later, he knocked at my door again. Upon arriving at his office, he had work that claimed his attention, and he had not made the call to his sister. However, later in the morning, he received a telepnone call from her, advising him that their brother's wife had been instantly killed in an automobile accident. Something had been trying to reach Paul and had not been totally successful in manifestation.

These same powerful forces are yours to claim dynamically in your life. Learn to use them and they will work magnificently for you.

Now that you are aware of extra "tools" at your disposal, let's start using them to work with the prosperity idea of building a treasure map, using your Macro-Mind Powers of Telepathy, Clairvoyance and Precognition, and Natural-Sensory Perception!

The Macro-Power of Pen on Paper!

Occasional wishing, or a half-hearted wanting cannot form the perfect connection or communication with your omnipotent Macrocosmic Power! You must be earnestly truthful and sincere in desiring certain conditions or things, whether they are mental, physical, or spiritual.

And remember! BE SPECFIC!

If you want an automobile, decide what kind, price, style, color, size, and all the other details, including *when* you want it! If you want a new home, picture the structure, the grounds, and see it tastefully furnished. Picture the kind of lot the house will be placed on, decide how much it will cost.

If you want money, write down the amount and see it coming to you debt-free from universal substance. If you want to break a record in your business, write it down, and write the date you would like to achieve this goal. List your prospects and their potentials.

This might seem foolish at first, but you can never realize your desires completely if you don't know positively and in detail what you want and when you want it! If this is hard for you to decide, then perhaps you need to be more in earnest about the whole thing.

YOU MUST BE DEFINITE, and when you are, your results will be surprising and almost unbelievable.

GET DEFINITE ABOUT PROSPERITY,
SO PROSPERITY CAN GET DEFINITE ABOUT YOU!

The Incredible Impact of Picture Power!

This amazing Treasure Mapping Method of securing what you want applies to *everything you are capable of desiring.* Since the scope of its tremendous outworking is so great, I suggest that you first treasure map for those things with which you are most familiar, such as an amount of money, some personal accomplishment, or the possession of some material thing. These desires are more easily and quickly obtained than the discontinuance of a fixed habit, the welfare of others, or the healing of mental or bodily ills.

Picture Power carries an incredible impact. When you place your treasure map where you can see it daily, you are offering your mind a super-fantastic opportunity to be productive! This wonderful picturing power of the mind is being discovered by psychologists who say that imagination is one of our strongest mind powers.

I'm sure you can recall seeing pictures of carvings on the walls of caves done by prehistoric man of the food he hoped to obtain. He believed that if he looked at these pictures often, some great unseen power would bring the food near him in the form of game, fish or fowl.

The Egyptians also used the picturing power of the mind with artwork in the tombs of their pharoahs. When a royal child was born, his tomb was immediately started. In this tomb, pictures were painted showing all the experiences he would have throughout his life . . . a happy life, victorious achievements. And the Egyptians fully believed these pictured events would come about in the life of the royal child.

The Grecians surrounded their prospective mothers with elegant statues and beautiful pictures and lush scenery so that the unborn children would receive the benefits of health and beauty from the mind-pictures of the mother!

The picturing power of your mind transforms your thinking from "Oh, I can't have that!" into an attitude of "This is what I want and it is mine to claim!"

YOU CAN HASTEN YOUR GOOD BY PICTURING IT!

Creating Prosperity Through the Spoken Word

Any person who isn't aware of the power of the spoken word is living in the dark ages!

When you first list all your desires on paper, and then picture them in a treasure map, you start creating your good on the invisible planes of the universe. You start gathering the "gold dust" substance of the universe together in a momentum of specified activity. *But when you speak the word of prosperity, the vibrations of your words then move on that invisible substance, form it into definite results, and herald its birth in the visible world of matter.*

If you desire greater prosperity to come your way, speak the definite words that will bring it to you. SPEAK DEFINITE WORDS! Never think that a general affirmation will produce a specific result in your life. The laws of the universe don't work that haphazardly!

A woman I know went from a $6,000 a year secretary to a $10,000 a year department manager within eight weeks when she began affirming prosperity into her life! Here's her affirmation:

> **The Divine Substance of the Universe is all around me. I speak the word for the Divine Universal Substance to manifest in my life in the form of a better job with less working hours, more money, and greater personal fulfillment.**

Every single spoken word carries tremendous power, and that power is increased through the intensity of the feeling you place behind the word. *When positive words are combined with a powerful statement of affirmation, tremendous vibrational forces are set into motion which act as an influential magnet and profoundly affect Universal Substance and produce results.*

Fantastic miracles can be worked in your life by affirming words of prosperity aloud for just ten minutes a day!

Here are some starter prosperity affirmations that will work for you:

1. **The Universe is my source of supply and my unlimited substance is abundantly being manifested NOW!**
2. **I have a large, steady, dependable, permanent, happy, financial income NOW!**
3. **I am constantly surrounded by Divine Universal Substance and this substance richly manifests for me NOW!**
4. **My rich good is coming to me NOW, speedily, through both known and unknown channels!**

What Is a Treasure Map?

A Treasure Map is *pictured prayer*—the prayer of your heartfelt desires. It is made on a large sheet of paper or cardboard by pasting on it words, titles, or pictures clipped from magazines and newspapers to illustrate your sincere desires.

Treasure Mapping is somewhat like playing a game—a game of the universe with an enormous reward!

> WHEN YOU MAKE A TREASURE MAP, YOU PUT DOWN ON PAPER A PICTURE OF THE LIFE YOU WANT TO LIVE AND WHAT YOU EXPECT TO BE A PART OF THAT LIFE!

You will enjoy thinking about, preparing, and using your Treasure Map. And while you're doing these things, you're setting into motion amazing cosmic energies.

What Treasure Mapping Can Do for You

Treasure Mapping encourages you to *think* about your desires, which, in turn, enables you to clarify your thoughts and decide what you really want. As you keep your goal constantly before you, your Treasure Map stimulates your thoughts and opens your mind to new ideas which can help you obtain your goals. By directing your thoughts along positive lines, a treasure map helps you take advantage of the opportunities which come your way. It helps to give you confidence and courage to try out new ideas and expand your vision.

How To Make a Treasure Map

1. Decide what you want—what qualities you need, how you can improve yourself and your present circumstances to obtain your goal, what you wish to become, to do, and what you presently have for which you are grateful.
2. Clip words, titles, and pictures from magazines or newspapers to represent your desire and to help you achieve it. Try to find things that are in living color for this makes your treasure map more complete.
3. Select a sheet of paper or cardboard large enough for a background and paste your clippings on it. Use a pink background for love; a yellow background for illumination; a gold background for financial prosperity; a blue background for spiritual growth and attainment; and a green background for healing.
4. Hang your Treasure Map where you can see it often, but not where others might riducule or question your desires.

How to Use Your Treasure Map

1. Read your Treasure Map at least once daily, feeling the realness of your expressed desires, and try to live your life in accordance with it.
2. Accept and use the related ideas that come to you as you review your statements and affirmations on your Treasure

Map. Follow through with any ideas which come if at all possible.

3. Praise and thank the Universe each day for your present abundance. Every single atom in the Universe responds to praise and gratitude. Let these mighty atoms respond to you!
4. Do whatever you can each day to achieve your desires.
5. Give as much of yourself in loving service as you can each day.
6. Use every opportunity that comes your way to learn new things, new work, or strive to do your present work in a better way.
7. Be as happy as you can each day. Happiness is contagious, and can spread to everyone around you.

Do's and Don'ts of Treasuring Mapping

1. DO watch your thoughts and feelings and actions and strive to keep them aligned with your targeted goals.
2. DO give Treasure Mapping a fair test. Be sincere and try faithfully to live your desires.
3. DO make a new Treasure Map when necessary. When your old map no longer expresses your current desires, or when your desires have been fulfilled and you wish to move on to bigger and better things, discard the old one and prepare a new Treasure Map.
4. DO Treasure Map for what you *really* want. DON'T Treasure Map for a used car if you really want a sleek new car. DON'T Treasure Map for a secretarial job if you really want to be in management. *Be true to your real desires.*
5. DO live your Treasure Map to the best of your ability in keeping attuned and balanced with circumstances, wisdom, good judgment, and practicality.
6. DON'T allow discouragement or impatience to dilute or dissolve the faith, power, and forward movement you have initiated by preparing your Treasure Map.
7. DON'T be overzealous or dominated by the attitude that you must do it alone. You have a part in the fulfillment of

your desires and your part will be revealed to you through your precognitive powers. Your first step is to build or prepare your own consciousness for increased good.

8. DO place the words, "THIS OR SOMETHING BETTER" at the bottom of your Treasure Map. This prevents your limiting your good to your exclusive thoughts and allows the universe the opportunity to bring in a better abundance if it is for your greater good.
9. DO remember to place the words, "Thank you, Universal Substance" at the bottom of your map.

How a Mental Picture Produced a Million Dollars!

Helen H. is a mother of three children who lives in Texas with her husband, and has a firm belief that each person can improve the conditions of his life through the proper use of mental power. Helen's affirmation is simply, "Name it and claim it!" And she does! Since the beginning of this new awareness, Helen has named and claimed sports equipment, electric appliances, a Hammond organ, trips to New York, Washington, and Europe, and in 1966, she won a $50,000 home in a contest sponsored by the Formica Corporation!

By way of explanation for her good fortune, she states, "I don't believe in luck, and I don't believe in accidents. *I simply project my goal on my mental screen. Then I give it nothing but positive energy.*"

This is not wishful thinking; it's a fact. You can accomplish the same thing, for you, too, can tap the well-spring of Macrocosmic Mind Power and Energy. If you give your wishes and desires enough energy, *they will manifest!*

How to Go the "Extra Mile"

Keep in mind that your pictured good will come into manifestation *as fast as your subconscious mind can accept it!* If you have been a "negative thinker," or an "I can't have," person, your pictured good may seem so vastly different from what your mind is accustomed to experiencing that it takes some time for the subconscious to absorb this new way of thinking and decide you really mean business about being prosperous!

This is where persistence pays off. *Hang in there!* Go that "extra mile" in holding on to your desires, and your faith in its perfect outpicturing.

Remember the importance of being clear and concise in your picturing. If your pictured good seems slow in coming, it could be because you have cluttered your mind with too many abstracts or too many pictures, or you may be trying to produce too much too fast.

A one-man craft shop cannot produce the same quantities as an assembly-line factory. Take one step at a time. Do your *thinking clearly.* Do your *contemplating wisely.* Do your *deciding definitely.* Do your *picturing positively and powerfully.* Clarify your desires and picture what you most need and want in the beginning steps of Treasure Mapping. This will open up the way for picture power to produce—and quickly.

Your Personal Universal Plan for Success

DARE TO LET GO OF ALL LIMITATIONS.

Remember that only you, yourself, can set any kind of limit on yourself. Stop saying that you've had a hard time in life. Stop talking about unhappy past experiences. Stop trying to get sympathy. Who needs it!

As long as you do this, you are still emotionally attached to that difficult experience. You are continuing to feed it emotionally. You are keeping limits on yourself, and there is no room in your thoughts and feelings for a better experience!

And don't let others place limitations on you! I'll share a personal experience with you that is typical of the mind-meddling, prosperity-blocking attitudes that can come to you from others.

It seems that a time inevitably descends into every well-organized life when the props are pulled from under your air of self-assurance and you accept your share of hard knocks and cheerfully grin and bear it. But oh, the perils that befall a budding young writer!

I'm beginning to believe that writers should be like old radio heros and heroines—heard but never seen—and then they could be anything the reader's imagination created. An incident at a supermarket several years ago (during my budding, "By God, I'll do it!" days) dealt a shattering blow to my ego.

I was struggling to navigate the four-wheeled monster called a shopping cart down the canned goods isle when I almost ran down my next-door neighbor. An out-of-town guest was along, and Lynn (God bless her) introduced me as a writer.

I grinned, smoothed my blue denim skirt, stood a couple of inches taller in my macrame wedgies.

The woman's eyes widened. "A writer!" she exclaimed. "But you look like a plain old housewife!"

Now how do you answer a remark like that? A housewife! And I wasn't even married! I never learned what she thought writers looked like, but apparently I was a sad disappointment. I wanted to cry, but my mascara would have run!

Yet, I could emphathize with her. She must have felt the same way I did when I discovered H. G. Wells didn't have a scientist's beard!

Most people envision a writer as a unique person of mystery, living in a world of fantasy, far removed from everyday indulgences. I conceived writers should be weird and extremely unconventional. They could be wildly exciting, stimulating, and unpredictable. But pushing a grocery cart? No! It was too much for the lady to comprehend.

As my neighbor and her guest wandered away, I wanted to rush after that poor woman, clutch her arm, and restore her faith by proclaiming, "I DO carry a portable typewriter in my car. I DO have an auburn wig for important interviews when my hair's a mess. I HAVE conversed with presidents in person. But it was too late. She was gone.

If she ever thought of me again as a writer, she probably remembered a "plain old housewife" in sweater and skirt, pushing a grocery cart . . . and she'd never want to identify with that!

However, I could not allow her idea or impression to become a limitation to me. *I knew who and what I was, and that was what truly mattered.*

You are learning more of *who* and *what* you are also. Now get going toward becoming even greater than you already are!

A Word of Caution

A wise teacher once said, "Be careful what you wish for and desire; it will come to live with you!" This is true. So, be careful when asking the Universe for a specific desire and claiming Macro-Power to help you achieve it. *Yes, it is possible to want and obtain that which will make you miserable.* You can have what you want, but you must take all that goes along as part of the package.

Therefore, in planning your desires, plan only that which you are sure will give to you and your fellow man the greatest good here on earth. By doing this, you will be paving the way to that future hope beyond the vale of human understanding.

"This, or something better!"

MACRO-MIND "TREASURE MAPPING" MOTIVATORS!

1. Get definite about prosperity, so prosperity can get definite about you.
2. Picture what you want!
3. The utter and outer have a similar base. What you utter becomes outer in your world. Speak positive, powerful, prosperous words.
4. I have heard it estimated that spoken words of prosperity can speed up your results by as much as eighty-five percent.
5. Macro-Mind Power not only works—it's natural and normal!
6. Mind has no limitation in time and space!
7. Like always attracts like in the realm of mind!
8. A Treasure Map is pictured prayer—the prayer of your heartfelt desires.
9. A powerful way to create your prosperity mentally is by picturing it, first in your mind, then transferring this mental picture to paper as a Treasure Map.
10. Results are not produced by generalities because generalities lack creative substance and power. Vague hopes and dreams do not convince your subconscious. But a clearcut, precise picture of your desire activates people, places, and events into cooperation with your pictured prayer—your desires!
11. You can picture your way to increased prosperity in whatever way you desire—world travel, money, health, fame, harmony, love, friends!

12. Use your macro powers of telepathy, clairvoyance and precognition, and natural-sensory perception to "tune in" to your greater good and help you take the proper steps in bringing it into manifestation in your life!

6

How Macro-Mind Power Can Influence Others in Your Behalf

Undoubtedly the most sought after of all the wants of people everywhere is REAL PERSONAL POWER—*Self-Power stemming from an endless reservoir flowing within the individual.* Some people seek diligently, discover, and learn to use this tremendous power. Some find it, only to lose it quickly; others never uncover its secrets. In this last category of seekers, some become so obsessed with the intense desire for obtaining this power that the futile seeking of it drives them to madness.

You have a natural and strong desire to obtain *Real Personal Power*. You have a normal appetite for genuine Self-Power. And that is good! Everyone who seeks Self Power searches not only for its amazing secrets, but also *searches for a simplified and practical means for achieving it quickly and surely.*

Regardless of how little or how much of *Real Personal Power* you desire, *whatever degree you achieve will contribute toward a richer, fuller, and more satisfying life.*

Occasionally, you may have felt that you were standing aside while less-worthy persons acquired greater power. You no longer need to stiffle your ambitions. Self Power, influence, and control of your life are as great a potential within you as in anyone. No one has an "advantage" over you! That same power potential swells grandly within you. Simply *find* your want, get the "*feel*" of it, and *tune in* to and *use* the copious energy of Macro-Mind Power to achieve your desires.

How You Can Play A Star Role in Life

Dear Friend, LIFE IS YOUR TOOL! You are living in the greatest scientific and spiritual age in the history of mankind.

YOU ARE LIVING IN THE AGE OF MIRACLES, AND MIRACLES ARE HAPPENING!

Today, what man can conceive, man can achieve! Surely, the art of successful living is the greatest of all sciences. Following the Laws of Universal Truth, and using the mighty force of Macro-Mind Power in daily practice, you can become phenomenally successful in anything you direct your mind toward achieving.

What is the mystical ingredient that causes one person to become a famous celebrity, and another—with apparent equal abilities—to remain unknown throughout his life? The answer is quite simple:

THE PERSON WHO STEPS FORWARD AND SHINES AS A BRILLIANT STAR IN LIFE IS THE PERSON WHO BELIEVES IN HIMSELF AND HAS FAITH IN THE OUTWORKING OF UNIVERSAL LAWS!

What are you attracting to yourself at this very moment? Do people recognize you when you enter a room? Do heads turn and admire your radiance when you walk down the streets? Have you been recognized by the community in which you live as having contributed worthwhile activities to its growth and development? Or, are you anonymous, and no one notices when you pass? If the latter is true for you, reverse this situation immediately by *starting to use what you already have,* and thereby, through the Law of Use attract additional ability, thus *increasing your competency to perform.* You can begin *right now* making use of your talents to their fullest potential.

Adopt the following classic lines immediately as a success formula for developing REAL PERSONAL POWER.

Lose this day loitering—'twill be the same story
Tomorrow—the next day more dilatory.
Then indecision brings its own delays.
And days are lost lamenting over days.
Are you in earnest? Seize this very minute—
What can you do, or dream you can, begin it.
Courage has genius, power, and magic in it.
Only engage, then the mind grows heated.
Begin it and the work will be completed.

Goethe

How to Make Your Influence Felt by Others

Have you ever stopped to realize that most people are psychic? It's true! And by this, I mean that almost every person you meet is *sensitive to the thoughts and feelings of other people.* Everyone has capacity to "tune in" and feel the mental vibrations constantly being generated and broadcast from within you as well as from others.

You are psychic! Have you not felt intensely the uneasiness stemming from being in the presence of someone who gave vent to a violent outburst of anger? Your instinctive reaction was the desire to remove yourself immediately from this person's angry presence. On the other hand, have you not found yourself in the presence of someone who exuded a deep sense of serenity and peace? You enjoyed the vibrations of calmness and serenity projected from this person's presence.

Vibrations are powerful messengers, and they carry the message true.

> YOU CANNOT FEEL ONE THING AND TRULY PROJECT ANOTHER.

Vibrations are like electric currents—qualified by whatever button you push! When you feel serene and confident, this same vibrational attitude is projected to all who come within your sphere of existence. When you question your abilities, and insecurities rear ugly heads, this vibrational attitude is projected to people. The more secure and important you feel as a person, the stronger will be the feeling of poise and self-importance that will be felt by others with whom you come in contact.

When your activities are constructive, outstanding, unusual, and powerful, your personal influence will be felt by others. They will desire to accomplish what you have achieved. *Success begets success! Like attracts like! As in mind, so in manifestation!* Truth adages? You'd better believe it!

As you grow in personal self-esteem, people of prominence and influence will become attracted to you and will desire to include you in their circle of friends. Glorious new doors of opportunity will open to you and make it possible for you to enter into a magnificent life, both professionally and personally.

How You can "Shine Like the Sun"

Recently, my husband and I were enjoying a marvelous dinner at Peaks of Otter Lodge, a beautiful resort hotel nestled in the Blue Ridge Mountains. Although the restaurant buzzed with activity, and the waiting time to be seated was almost an hour, we knew the food and atmosphere were worth experiencing.

While waiting for a table, Michael and I stopped along the shore of the beautiful lake, and *every single person who passed us smiled a greeting!* Many spoke briefly to us, and some stopped to chat, but *every person acknowledged our presence in an outward manner!*

When we were called for dinner, the hostess seated us at a lovely table, in a prominent position by a window overlooking the lake. Service was prompt and courteous. Michael and I were about thirty minutes into our dinner and thoroughly enjoying ourselves. We were discussing new Macro-Mind ideas for an upcoming Biofeedback seminar Michael was to conduct aboard an ocean cruise. Our sharing was animated and excited. We were so totally involved with our conversation that we were oblivious to others in the restaurant until I felt a gentle hand upon my shoulder.

I turned and looked into the smiling eyes of a woman in her forties. Her husband stood by her side, smiling at us, and she said, "I was *compelled* to come and speak with you! *Who are you?*"

I replied with my name. She shook her head. "No, that's not what I mean. You are someone very special. The people at our table have been observing you and your husband from the moment you entered the room. *There's a beautiful golden glow about you, and I have never seen such a happy face in my life!*"

I was somewhat surprised, but she clasped my hand and I thanked her for expressing her feelings. She looked into my eyes again and asked, "Will you please give me a blessing so some of your radiance can flow to me?"

A couple of moments passed as I silently held her hand in mine, and then I told her some of the things I'm sharing with you in this book. I shall never forget that lady, for her actions and her presence said to me, "*Yes, you are letting your light shine brightly!*"

You know that by using shoe polish and a little effort, you can put a dazzling shine on your shoes. This same analogy applies to your personality. *Apply the polish of courtesy and consideration to your activities and it will cause your personality to sparkle. Apply the supra-polish of radiant thought impressing your subconscious mind, coupled with extra-strength FAITH, and your personality will scintillate like a brilliant diamond!*

How Mike L. Attracted Good Fortune

I was on a business trip to Denver and shared a seat on the plane with a remarkable young man. A congenial fellow, Mike expressed that he was unhappy with his commitment in the Air Force because his true desire was to study drama and become an actor and a dancer. In order to uplift his spirits, I gave him the basic principles of the laws and use of Macro-Mind Power. After arriving at my destination, I did not see Mike again.

Several months later, I received a telephone call from Mike. He had absorbed every word I had spoken to him and *decided to take action.* He counseled with his commanding officer in the Air Force, stated his honest feelings, and requested a discharge from services. Within a month, Mike received a general discharge based on honorable circumstances! For about a month after his discharge, Mike lived in limbo, but he held on to his dream. This is his story:

"After my discharge, I found a small efficiency apartment and obtained a job as a designer in a florist while I regrouped my thoughts and retargeted my goals. All the things you told me flashed like neon signs through my mind, and I believed and somehow knew that good things were happening in the ethers, preparing to descend into material manifestation. I thought often of the richness and goodness of the Universe, and spoke aloud my desires to be showered with the abundance of its substance. I imagined myself to be rich in mind, rich in health, rich in financial abundance, and rich in the opportunity to do what I wanted most to do.

"I KNEW POSITIVELY THIS WAS THE TRUTH ABOUT MYSELF!

"Within three weeks, I enrolled in the Denver Concert Ballet. Two weeks later, I was offered a full scholarship to study drama and ballet. What joy! My dream is manifesting, and my first role is that of playing the demon in 'Firebird.'

"I now have an opportunity to meet some of the world's finest

dancers and am working hard to perfect myself and my talents so I will be ready for action when the BIG opportunity comes!"

You can create this same atmosphere of rich abundance in your life. Be certain to include in your Master Plan the desire to attract abundance of health, wealth, and happiness. See your cup filled to overflowing with all the good the Universe has to offer. Desire to receive all these things. Imagine yourself starting to receive them right now in great abundance. Realize you will receive your heart's desires—and they will magnetically be drawn to you.

How To Develop Macro-Mind Magnetic Expression

Question: *How can I develop a radiant and sparkling personality?*

Answer: *You can LET the real YOU express itself in and through you.*

Unfold the real magnetic YOU into a charming and dynamic presence that is greatly admired.

YOU CAN UNLEASH THIS TREMENDOUS POWER OF YOUR MIND AND ALLOW IT TO WORK FOR YOU TOWARD GAINING MAGNETIC PERSONALITY.

People delight in the charm of your Real Self, and you will become a very much liked, respected, and popular person.

Socrates, the Greek philosopher, knew and stated an important rule for acquiring a radiant personality. He said simply,

"MAN, KNOW THYSELF!"

It was the great Shakespeare who gave us the basic rule for obtaining and maintaining a radiant, magnetic, self-expressive personality. From one of his immortal plays we take the power-packed line:

To thine own self be true, and it must
follow as the night the day, thou canst
not then be false to any man.

When you realize your *genuine true worth* as an individual of the Universe; when you put your many talents to work, when you take action to become even greater than you are already, then *you start being true to yourself!*

BEING TRUE TO YOURSELF REQUIRES THAT YOU HAVE RESPECT FOR YOURSELF AS AN INDIVIDUAL AND HAVE RESPECT FOR OTHER PEOPLE.

It means being polite, courteous, and friendly in your everyday contact with all persons you meet. Remember, every single person has the same right to live life abundantly as do you. Through this powerful realization, you can become a fantastic ambassador of good will wherever you may be. And in accordance with the Law of Cause and Effect, people will give back to you the respect you lovingly give to them.

How to Implement a Seven-Day Macro-Mind Improvement Program for Exerting Greater Influence over Others

I've mentioned to you before that what you do repeatedly becomes a habit. Here is a simple, workable method for increasing your influence over others through gaining a magnetic personality. For your great benefit, make it a "must" to practice the following mental activities for *seven full days* and you will become a glowing person with a radiant new personality.

1. As you are getting dressed each morning, *look into your mirror and give yourself a great big SMILE!* Then, say to yourself, "I look wonderful. I feel wonderful, for this is a glorious day! For the precious time allotted me this day, I am going to act in a courteous, charming, and magnetic manner!"
2. Greet the first person you meet, and every other person you come in contact with during the day, with a happy sounding "Hello!" *Inject a ring of good cheer* into your voice and let it live with you thoughout the day.
3. *Truly listen to what each person you meet has to say.* Let a sincere, interested expression be your constant companion. Speak gently and kindly when you meet and part. Let the person know you really care about him.
4. Take a "quiet time" when convenient for you during the day to sincerely affirm the following statements:

   I am today and every day becoming a more attractive person in every way."
   I am today radiant, happy, carefree. I know myself.

I am sincere and friendly to everyone I meet today.
I will today make a good impression wherever I may be.
I will today maintain respect for myself and for others.
I will today radiate personal charm.

5. When you arrive home each evening, look into your mirror and say to yourself, "*Today has been a glorious day in which I have expressed myself, to the best of my ability, in a charming and sincere and magnetic manner. I am happy.*"

Now, prepare a check chart for yourself on a plain piece of paper so you can monitor your progress. Give yourself one check mark for each day you practice this method. Prepare your check chart as shown below:

MACRO-MIND MAGNETIC EXPRESSION CHECK CHART							
1. Sun.	Mon.	Tues.	Wed.	Thurs.	Fri.	Sat.	Total
2.							
3.							
4.							
5.							

How To Gain Tremendous Self-Confidence

I would be less than honest with you if I did not tell you that although you have amazing power to attract any good thing to you, *there are certain steps you must take in order to accomplish your desire*. It is important to know exactly what is keeping you from making the progress you desire, should this be the case.

Personal X-ray

- Do you habitually feel sorry for yourself?
- Do you hesitate overly long when making changes in your life?

- Do you lack the faith in yourself to do something really great?
- Does laziness cause you to fail to put forth needed effort to do something worthwhile with and for yourself?
- Do you fear what people may say if you move out of the rut you've made for yourself?

ALL OF THESE STATEMENTS ARE SUCCESS-CRIPPLING HABITS THAT CAUSE ROADBLOCKS TO THE INFLOW OF YOUR ABUNDANCE.

The greatest antidote for any of the above success-cripplers is to *count your blessings daily*. You cannot be aware of the abundance you have already received, and feel deprived at the same time. Free yourself from your own self-imposed bondage. Free yourself from self-condemnation. Such mental practices can offer you nothing but a feeling of despair. And you don't need, or deserve, that attitude!

START TO BELIEVE IN YOURSELF AND IN YOUR POWER OF ATTRACTION!

It is true that if you don't believe in yourself, no one else will! *You can do anything you make up your mind to do. Remember, you attract to you what you think and believe.*

Self-confidence makes you a more interesting and attractive person. And best of all, the more you believe in yourself, the more power you possess to attract your good.

A Macro-Exercise To Stimulate Self-Confidence

Sit in a comfortable chair. Close your eyes and completely relax. For one minute, imagine yourself to be a very important person. For one minute, believe you are extremely important. *Know that no other person can do exactly what you can do, in the manner you perform.* Now, visualize yourself being very brave and courageous. Make a mental picture of yourself being very brave and confident and self-assured. Imagine yourself going through the day feeling calm, poised, and master of all you survey. Feel this truth about yourself and sustain this feeling for several minutes. Next, open your eyes, lift your head up high, and go forth fully convinced that you will enact the part of personal self-confidence throughout the day.

PUT INTO LIVING ACTION THE BEINGNESS THAT YOU ARE ALREADY EXPRESSING!

How Lewis A. Used Macro-Mind Power to Overcome and Eliminate Racial Prejudice And Acquire a Sincere, Lifetime Friend

Lewis A. recently related to me how he had made a major step forward in his understanding regarding people. He had grown up in a racially prejudiced home and, as a result, experienced difficulties in working with black people. Lewis' job with a government agency, however, brought him in contact with people from all races and nationalities—and Lewis's boss was a black man. The working relationship between the two men was strained, and both Lewis and his wife experienced ill health, financial instability, and family difficulties.

Lewis decided to dwell on a Positive Mental Attitude and began daily affirming:

There is only one Presence and one Power in all the universe—God, the Good—and this Presence and Power makes all people one in spirit.

As Lewis affirmed his oneness with all people, nothing spectacular happened, yet, things began to gradually improve. He could see that his relationships with people were evidently better in every phase of his life. His wife's health mended; the severe headaches Lewis suffered disappeared and he no longer needed the expensive medication so long prescribed. Lewis continued affirming his oneness with all people and his boss became increasingly warm and friendly and, after six months, recommended Lewis for an advanced position in his job. Lewis' total life prospered in ways he could not have foreseen.

How to Use Macro-Mind Power To Transform Enemies into Friends

I'm going to give you a dynamite-loaded truth!

YOUR PERSONAL ATTITUDES TOWARD PEOPLE WILL CAUSE THEM TO BECOME YOUR ENEMIES OR YOUR FRIENDS!

Perhaps this is shocking, but it is true. You have no place for enemies in your life plan. Emerson spoke wisely when he said, "To have a friend, be a friend."

A sure-fire secret for transforming a believed enemy into a friend is to be friendly to that person. If he refuses to respond in like manner, then release him from your life immediately. It might seem difficult at first to hold thoughts of Love for one who appears to be a foe, but it is important for you to remember that *there is no bitterness or hatred in Love. Love can overcome all seeming limitations or oppositions.* When you begin sending showers of Love feelings and thoughts toward one who seems inharmonious with you, your feelings of Love will be subconsciously felt in the heart of your opponent. His attitude toward you will then experience a change.

You can prove to yourself that this Macrocosmic method for transforming enemies into friends does work like magic.

How Deborah C. Used Macro-Mind Love Power to Overcome Hatred and Resentment

From Deborah's first meeting with Nancy, sparks literally blazed. There was no apparent reason for the fireworks, other than extremely different personalities, but Nancy seemed to delight in slinging hurtful remarks at Deborah. Inasmuch as the two girls shared classes together four hours each day, a problem loomed.

Deborah, being quite aware of the power of Macrocosmic Mind, decided to do something about the situation. She began to work with sending thoughts of love toward Nancy. Whenever Nancy's face would float before Deborah's mind, she silently sent thoughts of love, peace, and harmony.

Six months elapsed, and no visible results appeared. Then, both girls were given a special hospital work assignment requiring them to work together as a team for three months. *What an opportunity!* Deborah faced their first day as a team with mixed emotions. She truly wanted to be friends with Nancy, yet through her fleeting thought came the idea, "*But did the test have to be quite this demanding?*"

At the end of the first day's assignment, as the girls walked toward the seventh floor elevator in the hospital, Deborah took a deep breath and plunged into action. She stopped, looked at Nancy and said, "Nancy, I enjoyed working with you today. Can't we please be friends?"

She held out her hand to Nancy. For a few seconds, Nancy's face was immobile, and then it crumpled as tears flowed down her cheeks. Deborah put her arms around Nancy's shoulders and lead her to a quiet seat in a nearby visitor's lounge. Thoughts and feelings flowed from both girls like water over a dam. Nancy released her suppressed feelings of envy and resentment toward Deborah's tremendous talents and ease as a student. As both girls dried their tears, a new relationship emerged—a relationship of ease and calm and harmony. The two girls never became "buddies," but no longer did anger and resentment flare and cause discomfort.

How to Develop Faith in Yourself and in Others

Faith is a way of thinking, an attitude of the mind that gets amazing positive results. Faith is a conviction based on eternal laws and principles which never change, and which work equally well for all people. *The degree of workability depends on the degree of application of the individual.* Faith is the fusion of your thought and feeling, your mind and heart, which is so complete, inflexible, and impregnable that no external events or situations can move you.

Often in your life, you may see periods of formlessness, times of seeming confusion, when your precious ideas are in the embryonic stage and life may seem to be chaotic. But with patience and faith, what appears chaotic progressively evolves into a beautiful manifestation. What a tremendous comfort it can be to you to *know* that *you are ever evolving.* Infinite Macrocosmic Power is continuously working with perfect order and precision to propel you onward and upward in growth and success.

The seed of faith is already within you, begging to be released by the power of your cooperation with the truth of its Reality.

COMMIT YOUR WHOLE SELF TO *BEING* THAT WHICH YOU *ARE*!

You are blessed with the resourcefulness to meet and overcome any problems that life might offer. Faith provides strength and renewed energy to the executive faculty of your WILL and stimulates the Will to action. Take a look at your life. Where is it headed now? Are you going where you wish to go? Do you have the kind of friends you truly desire? Do you wield the influence in all areas of your life that you desire to wield?

Remember that strong convictions in your desires and unwavering faith are the parents of all the great and enduring achievements of the human spirit. Begin now to practice faith-thinking. This is not merely an intellectual process based on reasoning. You, as a faith-thinker, do not compare, analyze, or draw conclusions from known premises. You do not take appearances into consideration; you are not biased by precedent. *Your thinking gives form, without question, to ideas that come straight from the source—Macrocosmic Mind—and you have the power to succeed!*

How to Achieve Wonderful New Inner Security

How many people do you know who *really feel secure?* The feeling of security or of insecurity stems primarily from a basic approach to life. *If you are unfamiliar with your own innate greatness and the infinite riches within you just waiting to be unleashed, then you tend to magnify problems and difficulties which confront you.* You impart to these situations false powers and magnitude which you fail to attribute to yourself.

ONE OF THE PRIMARY REASONS FOR AN INSECURITY IS THAT YOU LOOK AT THE EXTERNALS OF LIFE AS *CAUSES*, INSTEAD OF REALIZING THAT THEY ARE MERELY *EFFECTS*.

The most important thing for you to do is to realize that *there is no separation from you and the omnipresent power of Macrocosmic Mind.* Upon applying the principles outlined for you in this book, you can develop a practical, workable, sane, and marvelous feeling of inner security. *Consciously join right now with the infinite power of Macrocosmic Mind.* The urge already screams from within you for reunion with this Eternal Source!

You are immersed in an infinite ocean of life—the power of Macrocosmic Mind. It constantly permeates the world in which you live, move, and have your being. *The moment you recognize Its existence, the power and wisdom of this infinite potential becomes potent and active in your life.* When this activity takes place, you will experience immediately a marvelous feeling of inner security, and discover the serenity and calm peace that floods your soul and keeps you ever master over all situations.

MACRO-MIND "INFLUENCING" MOTIVATORS!

1. A change in your attitude changes everything in your life. Become enthusiastic. Believe in yourself, and in your latent powers and abilities, and miracles will happen in your life.
2. Belief in false powers is your real problem. Real personal power is self-power stemming from the endless reservoir of Macrocosmic Mind flowing within you!
3. It is a monumental truth that people respect self-power but disdain and are unsympathetic toward all other power.
4. Your real personal power is an advantage no one else can match!
5. One of the primary reasons men and women fail to progress in life is their inability to get along with others. As you honor and respect others, the law of mind action brings honor and respect multiplied manyfold to you.
6. Lack of faith in yourself causes a lack of self-confidence. Developed faith in yourself produces inner security and great self-confidence.
7. You can develop self-confidence by believing in yourself and in the magnetic power of attraction of Macrocosmic Mind active within you.
8. Faith gives you the incentive, and courage gives you the power, to venture into new fields of adventure and develop them into gold mines of success.
9. Be true to yourself, and you cannot then be untrue to any man, woman, or child.
10. You can be happy if you look at the shining side of life. Hold no bitterness in your heart toward anyone. Remain cheerful and happy

in every circumstance and under every condition. Like people and love being with people. (Note: This is a whopping big undertaking! Can you do it!)

11. Say to yourself, "I feel wonderful today. I feel marvelous today. <u>This is going to be the happiest day of my life!"</u>
12. Faith is mental magnetism in action. Load your Mental Magnet and ignite its attracting power today!

7

How Macro-Mind Power Can Activate the Love Principle—Bringing Abundance in Your Life

The Irresistible Power of Love

When I was twelve years old, I attended a New Thought lecture with my parents and heard the speaker make a fantastic remark. It was, "When your heart is filled with Universal Love, you can never be critical or irritable, rather, *you will be divinely irresistible!*"

This remark crashed into my mind and made such a strong impression upon me that I've never forgotten it. And as the years passed and I encountered many opportunities to use the wisdom contained in this statement, its reliability has been proven over and over.

> WHEN YOUR HEART IS FILLED WITH UNIVERSAL LOVE, YOU CAN NEVER BE CRITICAL OR IRRITABLE, RATHER, YOU WILL BE DIVINELY IRRESISTIBLE!

Question: Well, first of all, what *is* Universal Love?

Answer: Universal Love is the pure essence of Macrocosmic Mind that binds together the entire human family. Of all the attributes of Macrocosmic Mind, Love is undoubtedly the most beautiful, the most important. Why? Because Love is the power that joins and binds in divine harmony the Universe and everything in it; Love is the great unifying and harmonizing principle known to man.

Charles Fillmore said that Universal Love is impersonal. It loves for the sake of loving. It is not at all concerned with *what* or *who* it loves, nor is it concerned with whether or not love is returned to it. Like the sun, its joy is in the shining forth of its nature.

LOVE IS AN INNER QUALITY THAT SEES GOOD EVERYWHERE AND IN EVERYBODY.

It insists that all is good, and by refusing to see anything but absolute good, it causes that quality finally to appear uppermost in itself and in all things.

Love Is the Great Harmonizer And Healer in Your Life

Whoever calls on Macro-Mind Power for healing is calling on divine Love. It will bring your own to you, adjust all misunderstandings, and make your life and affairs healthy, happy, harmonious, and free.

FACT: FROM ALL ETERNITY, PURE DIVINE LOVE HAS EXISTED AND WILL CONTINUE TO EXIST. GOD—MACROCOSMIC MIND—IS PURE LOVE, AND THE POWER AND CAPACITY OF LOVING POINTS TO THE EXISTENCE OF INNUMERABLE THINGS TO BE LOVED. THIS IS ONE OF THE GREAT SECRETS OF CREATION.

Several years ago, a business associate pointed out to me the tremendous success power of Universal Love. Harry's work involved constant contact with all shapes, sizes, and colors of people and personalities. He needed a key to successful communication with this kaleidoscope of associates. Then he told me how he developed his own private success formula for communication—especially with troublesome people.

When an important appointment was upcoming, he retired to his office, closed the door, and became still and quiet. He filled his mind with a mental picture of the person he was to interview and blessed him with an affirmation of love. Here is his affirmation:

I am a fantastic radiating center of Universal Love, mighty to attract my good, and with the ability to radiate good to others—especially ____________________ . (Here he said the name of the client.)

This action on his part generated an electric force to which both he and the client became attuned.

Remember that it isn't enough just to *verbalize the words. Feel* through the words you speak to reach the energy and the action they describe. *Feel* the power of Macrocosmic Love pulsing through you and your words with your heart, mind, soul, and strength. *Feel* this glorious divinity within, your True Self, responding like an unfolding flower to your interest, your desire, your attention, your appreciation, and your love!

We often hear about the success power of love. In his book "Love or Perish," Dr. Smiley Blanton stated that the greatest human need is the need for love, and that none of us can survive without it. Man must have love in his life in some form or he will perish.

Love Is the Greatest Power on Earth

Every single atom in the Universe responds and yields its deepest secrets to Macrocosmic Love. George Washington Carver loved the lowly peanut into a multimillion dollar industry!

There's nothing new about these ideas regarding the miracle-working power of love. The Greatest Teacher of the ages informed a young lawyer who came to see him that love was the greatest of all the commandments. And Paul, one of the world's greatest intellectuals and builder of early Christianity, attributed everything to the power of love!

An Esoteric Revelation About Love

From an early Christian manuscript comes a beautiful admonition:

> Nor can that endure which has not its foundation upon love,
> For love alone diminishes not, but shines with its own light;
> Makes an end of discord, softens the fires of hate, restores
> peace in the world, brings together the sundered,
> Redresses wrong, aids all and injuries none;
> And *who so invokes its aid* will have no fear of future ill,
> But shall find safety, and have everlasting peace.

Love is your personal "GO" light, while anything less than a loving nature is a definite "STOP" light!

Love is real. It works! Love is gentle, yet undoubtedly the strongest tool you have to work with. You are living and moving right now in this tremendous energy field. This Universal Love *responds to what you think* and you can use this amazing power to change any condition or circumstance in your life, regardless of how unchangeable the situation may seem.

Several years ago, I had an experience that proved to me there is definitely nothing weak about Love; that Love can overcome all obstacles; that Love can touch all people; that Love can win more battles than verbal weapons; and that Love is truly a "secret weapon" for right results.

I was asked to take a job for one year as the public relations director for a nonprofit organization. This position was *in addition to* my regular job as executive with a large furniture manufacturing organization. It was the kind of job that no one else wanted because it demanded a lot and offered little in the way of rewards other than, as I was told, "The joy of being of service!" Well, that and fifty-nine cents would buy a loaf of bread at the time!

But it was a challenge, and I agreed to assume the responsibility. At the first meeting with the planning committee, things didn't look too promising. One of the committee members objected to my position because "I was too young and inexperienced!" I agreed with the inexperienced analogy in this new area of work, but the "young" bit bugged me. After all, I had proven myself in other important areas. Another committee member mumbled a remark about "afraid of red heads being temperamental." Right then, I wanted to belt her, but remembered that wasn't the way Love worked. And I definitely had chosen the Universal Power of Love as my "secret weapon" to get this organization on its feet.

The presentation theme of my outlined activities for the organization's work in the community was based on the unifying, harmonizing power of Love. The goal was to pull the people of the community together in a major and meaningful project.

Immediately the committee member who objected to my youth and inexperience tried to shoot holes in my proposal. I remained calm and began repeating the love-blessing affirmation quietly in my mind and directing Love power toward him. Other committee members could see the logic and workability of the ultimate goal of the proposal and liked the overall idea. The objecting member became so upset that he resigned from the committee and stormed out of the office. I relaxed and breathed a sigh of relief. This was Love's first step in clearing away inharmony. The members of the committee paused and sent the departing man soothing thoughts of peace and calmness—and he never came back!

As work progressed, we opened each of our committee meetings with the affirmation:

> **Divine Love is working through us now to bring about a better community. Divine Love abundantly provides everything this organization needs to complete this special project. Divine Love is victorious NOW!**

The results of our weekly committee meetings and the effects of the work accomplished by the end of the year was almost unbelievable! As we poured forth thoughts, feelings, and words of universal love into the project, doors opened everywhere. Attitudes and actions of people with whom we worked were harmonious, cooperative, and peaceful. New people, new activity, new prosperity flowed into the organization and community leaders began to sit up and take notice of our activities. It was a time for rejoicing, for not only had the community prospered through the power of love in action, but the organization became more firmly established.

Although I am no longer actively involved with the organization, it has continued to grow and prosper and has achieved a new status of respect and appreciation in the community. Divine Love continues to do its perfect work with the group.

A Mental Love Magnet in Action

Your mind is a fantastic mental magnet. It can think an unlimited number of thoughts and translate these thoughts into mental pictures with the power of your imagination.

> THE IMPORTANT THING IS TO LEARN TO USE THIS MENTAL MAGNET EFFECTIVELY!

Ancient Truth—LIKE ATTRACTS LIKE!
Modern Formula—AS IN MIND, SO IN MANIFESTATION!

How does it work? Like this. Visualize thousands of tiny love-thought particles moving around in space. Each one is glowing with a brilliant light which emanates from its very core. Each love-thought particle is trembling violently with its unique vibrations and moving like a comet through space.

When two of these tiny love-thought particles bump together, they adhere, unite their vibration, tremble in unison, and continue in the orbit of the stronger vibration. These two love-thought particles may meet a third and fourth particle, and, joining with them into one larger trembling unit, move on until many love-thought particles are united. Other thought particiles which come close to this pulsating unit may tag along, or they may jump away repulsed. IT ALL DEPENDS ON WHAT TYPE OF VIBRATION THE MASTER UNIT CONSISTS OF!

A strong reaction is produced upon the thinker by the thoughts he generates. If your love thought is directed toward someone else, it flies like a well-directed missile toward that person.

Accept a word of advice here, please. NEVER PLAN RECKLESSLY, NOR TRY TO USE THE COSMIC UNIVERSE AS A PLAYGROUND. You are working with forces and energy which are tremendously powerful. Remember—as in mind, so in manifestation. Keep your motives high!

How to Develop Greater Love Capacity

Isn't it about time that you stopped fooling around with life and cheerfully admitted that there's one important thing you need to do? And you can do it! You can love God, love yourself, love life, love work, love play, love your friends, love your enemies, love your growing ability to love!

You've probably tried everything else—fear, condemnation, scheming, guilt, religion, education, science, manipulation, competing, warfare—everything the fertile human consciousness can invent to obtain your desires and most of these efforts have been found inadequate.

Now's the time to do the positive, guaranteed activity that will change this track record.

START LOVING!

Nothing less than Love can ever be as effective because you are created by Love, you live in Love, you are Love, and you are designed to love.

Over and over again people have defined Love and redefined Love. We have even redefined our definitions of Love and we didn't affect this magnificent power one bit. It just flows right on throughout the universe every minute of every day. So now take a positive step. *Cheerfully admit the most effective thing you can do is to love!* This realization clears the way for action. Positive action.

Stop all the defining, talking, searching, and START LOVING your way to prosperity in every area of your life. Know the truth about Love that sets you totally free from all restrictions and limitations.

Love is a miracle-worker. It takes the least desirable things and transforms them into objects supremely to be desired. An environment may be ever so unpleasing, but let Love pour its enchantments into the unhappy conditions, and joy and peace come into the situation and refashion it along lines of harmony and grace.

A group of people involved in a study group I was teaching worked with the power of Love in a prayer group activity and found it to be the greatest thing in the world to solve both personal and business problems. Once a week these people met for an hour and affirmed statements of Divine Love. Into these meetings they brought their private prayer lists of people and situations they wished to bless with the success power of Love. *No one else saw their prayer lists, nor did they talk about the people and problems their prayer lists represented.*

During each meeting they quietly held their prayer lists in their hands while they affirmed together various statements on Universal Love.

> DIVINE LOVE IS DOING ITS PERFECT WORK IN ME AND THROUGH ME NOW.
> DIVINE LOVE IS DOING ITS PERFECT WORK IN YOU AND THROUGH YOU NOW.

This particular group met for six consecutive weeks and affirmed these and other statements of Love repeatedly. Amazing things began to happen to various members of the group and to the people for whom they prayed. One woman, Patsy L., had been troubled for some time because of misunderstandings that had arisen a month previously between her and her teenage son. She had made every effort to reach Mike and recreate harmony and understanding, but she had been coldly rebuffed in spite of her loving efforts. So Patsy had been directing Universal Love Power toward this situation.

On the last night of the class, Patsy was driving home after the class had ended and heard what sounded like electrical crackles in the air. Startled, she thought something was wrong with her car and pulled to the side of the road and stopped. She inspected her car. Everything seemed in order, however, and she continued homeward. Suddenly, as she pulled into her driveway, a beautiful feeling of peace flowed through her and she felt an unusual excitement about arriving home.

As she opened the door to the entrance foyer, her son ambled out to meet her, grinned, and flung his arms around her embarrassedly.

"Hey, Mom, sorry I've been such a bum! You're pretty O.K., and I wanta be friends again!"

Patsy's response was to fling her arms about him and reply, "That's alright, Mike. Let's both release the past and go forward from right now."

He didn't see the moist tears in her eyes as she quietly gave thanks that Universal Love could dissipate negativity and heal the previous attitudes of misunderstanding and hostility.

How to Stop Heartache and Suffering

If a disturbing situation exists in your life and you want to put an end to that situation, then the normal approach is to study the situation. Look at it from all angles. If you are traveling on the highway and make a wrong turn, you study a map and get yourself *back on course* again. This is exactly what you must do with heartache and suffering. Study these emotions as carefully as any other condition you wish to correct.

You don't want temporary relief. You want to put an end to these undesirable conditions once and for all time. Why take an aspirin for temporary relief from a headache when you have the opportunity to destroy the cause of the headache? *It can be done.*

Question: What is suffering?
Answer: Suffering is pain caused by *wrong viewpoints* toward persons or situations or things. *You suffer when you become out of harmony with the Universe around you.*

A large hospital in Kansas City researched psychosomatic illnesses. The results of their research were amazing. One of the psychosomatic reasons listed for the common headache was "insecurity and a need for love." In the case of excessive overweight and overeating, one of the reasons listed was "a feeling of dissatisfaction with life and a need for love." And there were many other causes given.

The wonderful thing to be aware of and remember is that when there is a need for love, you can begin supplying this needed essence *immediately from within yourself.* You can let waves of love permeate every nerve and cell of your body.

A neighbor was healed of a painful back condition of long standing when she began releasing thoughts of Love from within herself by speaking words of Love to her body. Various treatments had been unsuccessful. Then she heard about the wonderful healing power of Universal Love. She began placing her hand over the painful area in her lower back, and visualizing undulating waves of light and love flowing into this area. She repeated the affirmation, "*I love you,*" over and over and really let a *feeling* of Love flow from her mind. The pain subsided after several Love treatments and gradually faded away.

Let Love Make You More Attractive

Have you met some person at some time or another, who, according to outer appearances, was not what you would term handsome or beautiful, yet who exuded a delightful inner beauty of spirit which fascinated you and attracted you to his company. You may have wondered what this person knew, what fantastic secret this person held that gave him such a dynamic inner charm.

It's easy to explain. That person had allowed the highest expression of the most effective emotion in life to live abundantly in his heart—Macrocosmic Love!

Macrocosmic Love can come radiantly alive in your heart also, and you, too, can radiate the effervescence of a dynamic inner charm. How? *Simply by loving all that is good with a heartfelt intensity and expressing that Love and kindness and caring to all people.*

You will be amazed at the transformation that will take place within you and in your world. Do this and you will become a kind-hearted person. Do this and you will attract new friends and companions and find a new relationship with old friends and companions. Do this and it will be impossible for you not to become an outstanding success. Why? *Because Macro-Mind Love Power is so great that it is like a giant magnet, attracting constantly the good in all persons, places, and circumstances into your life.*

Use the magnetic power of Love every day to draw to you all the good things necessary for your enjoyment of a rich and happy life.

How to Attract Your Life Partner

If you are currently a single person and have a strong desire to meet the "right" life partner, and *can* do something about this most important matter. You can use the laws of Macro-Mind Power to attract your right mate.

Let's use a simple, effective exercise.

1. Decide first that you wish to attract your right mate into your life and hold this thought in your mind firmly.
2. Next, take a plain piece of paper and make a list of all the desirable qualities you want in your perfect mate. Think of all the qualities you most admire and respect in a person of the opposite sex, such as a neat and attractive appearance, a sparkling personality, a strong, sound character, a sense of responsibility, someone who is mentally, physically, and emotionally compatible with your psyche, someone who is sexually compatible, and one with whom you would like to share your life. *Keep in mind that marriage is a union between two people of mind, spirit, and body.* Therefore, harmony in all areas is extremely important if you and your mate are to live happily together.
3. Now, go to your special "quiet place" where you can be

alone. Sit in an easy chair and completely let yourself relax. Close your eyes and visualize the kind of person you would like to marry. You've made your "desire list," so now visualize the Macro-Mind Power of attraction drawing this perfect person to you. Visualize that person and you becoming engaged. See the two of you being lavishly showered with wedding gifts and all kinds of well-wishes. Now, stretch your imagination and visualize the perfect wedding ceremony you have dreamed about. Visualize a happy wedding reception with friends you both know and enjoy. Finally, visualize the two of you leaving on an exciting honeymoon and picture yourself being happily married to that person for the rest of your life. *Believe this is true.* Feel the truth of this vision with all your being. It can be! Now, gently open your eyes, release the entire matter from your consciousness, and calmly go about your business with the certainty in your heart and mind that you will definitely meet your life partner.

4. Go out and *get involved* with people. You can't meet that "special person" tucked away in your own room, or apartment, or home. Put forth special effort. Live your life to the fullest. Accept invitations that come your way with the calm anticipation of meeting the right person.

This is an effective way to use Macro-Mind Power to attract your perfect partner. Practice this method each day. Now is the time to begin. You can achieve your heart's desire in the truth of Universal Principle.

A powerful affirmation for you to work with in attracting your life partner is this:

> **I am a radiating center of Universal Divine Love, mighty to attract my perfect life partner right now and live in happy togetherness for the rest of my life.**

How Love Protected a "Lost" Husband

A young woman telephoned me one night as I was working late in my office. Sue's voice was frantic. Her husband, Ray, had left for a business trip earlier in the day. He was flying his private plane and should have reported in several hours ago, but his flight plan had not been completed. He had taken off from the local airport on schedule, and was now more than two hours overdue at his point of destination.

Realizing that Sue's fear for her husband's safety had caused loss of control of her mental faculties, I began to talk with her in a calm, quiet manner. I gave her a Love-Light exercise to work with, and gave her instructions to start working with as soon as she hung up the telephone from our conversation. I asked her to take a picture of Ray in her hands; sit down, and concentrate upon his picture. I reminded Sue that Ray had been created in the image and likeness of God and that as a child of God, he was divinely protected. I asked her to close her eyes and visualize Ray surrounded by the warmth of their love and a beautiful and brilliant white light shield of protection. She was to hold that visualization for a couple of minutes and then to visualize his Cherokee Piper surrounded with the same beautiful and brilliant Love-Light shield of protection. I promised Sue that as she did this exercise, I would do the visualization along with her in my office.

She hung up the telephone with a trace of reassurance in her voice and said she would perform the exercise. Immediately, I began the visualization.

Two hours later, my telephone rang again and Sue's relief-filled voice poured across the wires. Ray had experienced inclement weather along with a mechanical problem with his single engine airplane. Because of extremely poor visibility, he had gone off course and because of the engine problem, he had to make an emergency landing. Fortunately, he had located a small private landing strip and was able to bring the plane down safely. But it took time to get help and to locate someone who could repair his aircraft. Realizing that Sue would be concerned, Ray had telephoned her as soon as he had everything under control and had the opportunity. When he talked with Sue, Ray related to her that as he was anxiously scanning the terrain below, trying to locate a place to land, he suddenly experienced a deliciously warm feeling of being wrapped in a soft, warm blanket of love and he immediately knew that everything was going to be all right.

Here was a living miracle, brought about by a young woman's love and devotion for her husband.

How to Control Your Emotions

Have you ever tried to ride a wild horse that has never been ridden? I watched a friend of mine try to do this and discovered an important secret. Until Lavon gained control of the horse, it bucked and reared, unseating him and hurling him to the ground. But repeatedly Lavon got up, brushed himself off, and climbed on the horse's back again. Finally, after much effort and expended energy on the part of both man and horse, man gained control.

This same thing is true about you. Unless you learn to control your emotions, they will control you and you will be tossed about and thrown, experiencing bruises that require time to heal.

Question: Just what is an emotion?

Answer: Emotion is a feeling, and feeling is external to thought. Behind every feeling or emotion lies a thought which is its direct cause. To erase or change an emotion, a change of thought is required.

UNWANTED EMOTIONS ARE FRUSTRATED FEELINGS OF UNEXPRESSED LOVE!

How many emotions are there? More than you can count! They run the gamut from the most gloriously sublime and peaceful to the most violent and harmful.

When something happens that causes a sudden intake of breath and you feel as if a missile hit you in the pit of the stomach, you're experiencing an emotion. When someone makes a snide remark that you "just happen" to overhear, and a warm rush of blood rises through your body, you're experiencing an emotion. When the person you love most in the whole world looks at you with frustration and stalks away in anger, and your heart sinks to the floor, you're experiencing an emotion. Then, you begin to think about the incident that happened, and start to roll around in the feeling that has overcome you, and it did just that—overcome you! When you concentrate upon the situation and the feeling, this situation becomes impressed on the subconscious part of your mind which is the powerful life force within you. This subconscious mind, then, reacts and causes you to feel the effects of what you have impressed upon it.

When you become emotionally upset about something, this strong feeling causes tension in every part of your body. This tension blocks the proper function of your body and its organs and pain and disease results. You may become mentally depressed and physically ill. On the other hand, when you experience a tremendous feeling of love, this greatest and most beneficial of your emotional gamut of capabilities will cause you to feel uplifted in spirit, and in addition, every part of your physical body will react to the harmony of the Macrocosmic Love feeling and function perfectly Both feelings—as different as June and January—are emotions.

Remember what was given you earlier—AS IN MIND, SO IN MANIFESTATION. If your thinking is calm and serene, then your feeling or emotion will be calm and serene. If your thinking has been of hostility, anger, fear, then your feeling or emotion will be of a violent nature.

But there is a way you can control your emotions.

1. When you feel the beginning of an unwanted emotion; when a thought regarding yourself or someone else, or an undesirable situation tries to enter your mind, blast it with a huge "STOP" sign. You can do this instantly, and it's a very effective method whether you're alone, or whether you're in a room filled with people. How?
2. You instantly replace the undesirable thought with a Macro-Mind Love Power thought. Psychologists tell us it's an impossibility for the mind to entertain two thoughts at the same time; its action is lightening quick—flashing from one thought to the other. Say to yourself quickly,

   "There is only one Presence and one Power active in my life—Total Good!"

   Repeat these words over and over to yourself as long as necessary for the unwanted emotional feeling to be dissipated. By taking this instantaneous action, you have made it impossible for the negative thought to enter your mind and set up housekeeping. YOU WILL HAVE GAINED CONTROL OVER WHAT WOULD HAVE OTHERWISE DEVELOPED INTO A NEGATIVE EMOTIONAL EXPERIENCE.
3. REMAIN CALM! Under all circumstances, maintain your composure and stay calm. Refuse to give power to anything.

Repeat to yourself,

"I am poised, peaceful, and calm through the power of Macrocosmic Mind which flows through me."

Close your ears if someone starts to criticize another. Keep your mouth shut if someone tries to be argumentative. Refuse to become involved if someone tries to entice you into the midst of juicy gossip.

YOU ARE THE MASTER OF ALL EMOTIONAL SITUATIONS IN YOUR LIFE. ACT LIKE IT!

4. Remember the old adage that "birds of a feather flock together!" It's true. *Make it your business to associate with harmonious people.* There are a lot of them in this world! Trouble-makers attract trouble and other trouble-makers. You don't need this useless, unnecessary suffering in your life.

How Love Will Make Your Dreams Come True

The Love you seek is also seeking you. Love is in your heart, at the very center of your being, and is an inherent part of you because you had your beginning in God, and God is Love.

It is wonderfully reassuring to realize that your desire for Love is but the *Love of Macrocosmic Mind in your heart seeking expression through you.* Every moment of your life becomes an opportunity to prove this Love by showing forth Love in all your thoughts, words, and deeds.

There is no need of your mind and heart that Macrocosmic Love cannot satisfy. There may be some experiences in your life that you find difficult to understand, but in every situation of trial or change, the power of Macro-Mind is working with you to strengthen, sustain, and guide you.

Do you doubt that your thoughts and words of Universal Love can have effective power in your own life and affairs? How could it fail—Universal Love is all around you.

One day a father and his young daughter climbed to the top of a high point of land overlooking the ocean on one side and a picturesque valley on the opposite side.

The father said, "Look up," and the child gazed into the vast expanse of the sky above.

"Look down," the father urged, and the child saw the reflections of white clouds and blue sky in the sea below.

"Look out," the father suggested, and his daughter looked and beheld the waves of water rolling over an infinite horizon.

"Now turn around and look over the green valley," he instructed.

As she contemplated the broad, beautiful landscape below, her father continued:

"My child, so high, so deep, and so wide is the Love of God for His children!"

With an insight characteristic of the childlike heart, the child softly whispered, "Daddy, if God's Love is so high, so wide, and so deep, then we are living right in the middle of it!"

The real quest of your soul is to experience the fullness of Universal Love. The results of Love are always good and crown your efforts with a success and riches that satisfy and enrich your life.

If you will take one faltering step toward acquiring a greater degree of Universal Love, it will rush to meet you and bear you on. When you seek to give or receive Love, you begin an experiment that ends as an experience. When you express Love, it transforms every facet of your life and draws to you associations and circumstances that flourish and grow into enduring and happy experiences. Quite often, your expression of Love may change the life of another, but it never fails to change your own heart and life.

You can love the Divinity within you into a radiant, healthy, rich, harmonious self-expression of Macrocosmic Mind. You are traveling the way of Love. Stay there confidently, joyously, enthusiastically!

The Rich Rewards of Love

1. Every single human relationship you experience can be a building block for a life of greater Love. The Macrocosmic Love Power is universal; it flows in all and through all.
2. Love is a state of spiritual understanding and elevated awareness. *To be real is to be loving.* To be considerate of others is to love with action. To be loving is to make contact with the supreme element of Macorocosmic Mind and ex-

perience success in every area of your life. You can literally *love your way to riches!*

3. Your love-capacity grows in leaps and bounds and develops spontaneously as you tune in to the power of Macrocosmic Mind.
4. Love is a miracle-worker in the field of prosperity. It has been estimated that only fifteen percent of a person's financial success is due to his technical ability while eighty-five percent is due to his ability to get along with people. And LOVE is the great harmonizer! Emmet Fox once wrote, "There is no difficulty that enough Love will not conquer."
5. Love is the creative energy that will free all mankind from every hang-up. Learn its tremendous secret potential for yourself, beginning *right now.*

A Bedtime Love Treatment

When it's the end of the day, and you're getting ready to retire, you can place a capstone of Macro-Mind Power atop your day's activities that will lay a great foundation for the next day. Here's how!

1. As you stretch out in your bed, consciously relax every muscle in your body. Mentally let go of every thought, every feeling, until your entire body is cradled and totally supported by your bed.
2. Now, reminisce over the day's activities. For every beautiful and meaningful event that transpired, give thanks to God for all the blessings you received. Maybe some of the day's activities were less than the perfection you'd like. Give thanks for these too, for they are fantastic harbingers of growth experiences.
3. *Feel Peace!* Imagine you are totally surrounded by an all-pervading essence of peace that permeates every part of your body. Feel this PRESENCE OF PEACE in your arms, your legs, your torso, your head. YOU CAN FEEL ITS EXISTENCE. Claim this wonderful peace as your divine heritage.
4. Now, in the cocoon of totally peaceful Macro-Mind Power, close your eyes and experience a marvelous night's sleep.

MACRO-MIND "LOVE" MOTIVATORS

1. Macro-Mind Power within me gives me the gift of Love. I accept this Love, and let it flow through me to bless my world, and make my life rich and harmonious.
2. There is no criticism nor condemnation in me, for me, or against me. Universal Divine Love is the law of my life, and harmony is now established in me and in all my affairs.
3. The Macro-Mind Power of Universal Love transforms my enemies into friends.
4. The Macro-Mind Power of Universal Divine Love sets me free from all financial worries.
5. Mighty currents of Universal Divine Love flow through me, healing my mind, my body, my affairs, making me whole and free.
6. I am utterly delighted by the new emerging self I see and feel coming to life in me and others.
7. I rejoice in the atmosphere of Universal Divine Love, forgiveness and growth that is being established in me and on the earth. I participate in it gladly.
8. I am a radiating center of Universal Divine Love, mighty to attract my perfect Life Partner and live in happy togetherness for the rest of my life.

8

How Macro-Mind Power Can Work Miracles of Healing

> The mind is hidden within the living matter . . . completely neglected by psychologists and economists, almost unnoticed by physicians. Yet it is the most colossal power of this world.

So spoke Alexis Carrel, noted scientist and medical doctor, during a lecture explaining how your body is enveloped with mind power which can be *directed and controlled.*

Our ancestors allotted great attention to the mysterious effect of man's mind upon his body. Metaphysical study attracted far greater men than did the study of medicine and aches and pains for many centuries. Ancient physicans attributed great importance to man's temperament and idiosyncrasies in connection with his physical health.

The Healing Secret of the Ages Revealed

> YOUR INDWELLING MIND POWER AFFECTS THE PHYSICAL HEALTH OF YOUR BODY.

Many fluctuating states of consciousness make your mind their home, *and each state of consciousness effects a corresponding organic expression in your body.* The power of your thought, energized by negativity, can generate organic lesions. *But you can be master of your thought, and master of the health of your body.*

When your activities are directed toward a precise, positive goal, your mental and organic functions become attuned and you experience radiant good health. If you wish to *maintain* this state of abundant health, you alone can impose upon yourself the desire to rule your mind.

What Happens When Imperfections Appear in Your Body?

Perfect health is a normal state of being. Disease is the unnatural state. Your beautiful body is intended to be healthy, harmonious, and perfect. *Imperfections occur in the body when the human mind is not fully cooperating with the perfect macrocosmic man.*

DISORDER IN ANY PART OF THE BODY INDICATES A WRONG ATTITUDE LIVING SOMEWHERE IN THE MIND.

The life forces in your body are normally nicely balanced, but this balance can be upset by worry, fear, anger or a multitude of other negative emotions.

Margaret M. is the picture of perfect health. At 64, she is active, alert, and vitally interested in life. I've never known Margaret to be sick in any way. She shared her secret affirmation with me for maintaining abundant good health:

Perfect Peace! The miracle of MACROCOSMIC MIND is at work in my body, mind, and soul. My life forces are peaceful and harmonious. There is no resistance in me against anything or anyone. My life is pure, peaceful. Mighty currents of universal healing love flow through me continuously, and I am kept whole and free.

You, too, can practice harmonious thinking and when you are able to maintain a quiet, peaceful, state of mind *under all circumstances,* you will not have to meet any more resistant conditions in your body.

Tell Your Body the Magnificent Truth About Itself!

Does it sound fantastic that you contain such remarkable and unlimited powers for physical renewal within yourself? Does it sound miraculous that you have the ability to deliberately release this power to go to work for you?

It's true! *To make whole is to cause that which has strayed from the divine idea of perfection—in function, in purpose, in action—to return to a state of agreement with this perfection.*

When the Master, Jesus, spoke commands to heal the sick and raise the dead, to love and to aid the suffering, He was simply issuing the only commandment that is necessary to bring all mankind back into the state of wholeness and at-one-ment with Macrocosmic Mind. BE THOU MADE WHOLE! Jesus used the Macro-Laser Light to cleanse and purify.

The healing concept is not restricted to any area or to anyone. Those who work in the midst of urban squalor, in poverty areas; those who work to lessen the devastation of racial strife and all forms of discrimination; those who work in their individual homes, are all healers. The surgeon who stands before an operating table is a healer. The mother who binds a child's cut is a healer. The metaphysician who directs thoughts of healing energy to another person is a healer.

> YOU ARE ALWAYS A PART OF A UNIVERSAL PROCESS OF HEALING AND MAKING WHOLE. REGARDLESS OF THE NATURE OF YOUR WORK, YOU CAN SEE AT LEAST A PART OF IT AS FULFILLING THE UNIVERSAL IMPULSE TO RIGHT WRONGS, TO USE GOOD JUDGMENT, TO FULFILL THE NEED FOR LOVE, AFFECTION, AND ACCEPTANCE.

Therefore, be aware. Talk to your body. Tell it the Truth about itself. Your body is eager to listen and know the great miracles it can perform!

Your Body's Twelve Healing Centers and How to Activate Their Vital Healing Forces

Another great healing secret of the ages is the truth that you have twelve dynamic mental powers, which are located in twelve vital nerve centers right within your body.

Right within your own body is found the center where life is generated! This life center is the fountain from which spring rivers of living waters. When your mind is focused in materialistic thinking, this fountain does not spew forth the pure, life-giving stream because it is dammed up by material thoughts about life. When you are quickened by the miracle of Macrocosmic thinking, the

Source of Life, the Waters of Life are set free and purified. *This healing Macrocosmic Life Energy completely transforms and renews the cells of your body.*

Is it surprising to you to learn that brilliant brain-thinking cells are located throughout your body? *This marvelous intelligence is waiting to be recognized and released for its healing mission!* In fact, when the pure truth is realized, your entire body is quite mental and thinks as you direct it to think! Ancient metaphysicians realized this truth, and references dealing with human beliefs and practices are found in some of our oldest documents. The ancient Greeks, Persians, Egyptians, and Hindus believed that every part of the body had a secret and important meaning, and religious leaders in these civilizations placed great statues of man's body within the secret chambers of their temples in order to study the body's hidden meaning and message.

Here are fantastic mind powers at your disposal *waiting to be used!* And they have been scientifically demonstrated!

At the turn of the century, a Yale University professor undertook to demonstrate the power of thought on the body. He suspended a young man in his laboratory on a perfectly balanced disk. The young man, a mathematician, was requested to think of some difficult problem in mathematics and try to solve it mentally.

As the student began to think intensely, the perfectly balanced disk tipped to the side where his head reposed. Blood flowing into the brain in increased amounts tipped the scale! Next, the professor requested the young man to think of running. The student was also interested in track, and as he began to think of running a hundred-yard dash in record time, the disk tipped toward the side where his feet and legs were. Blood was now flowing more freely into these organs of his body.

The displacement of the disk was greater when the professor asked the student to repeat the multiplication table of nine's than when he repeated the table of five's, which is an easier table!

The professor found that the center of gravity in the student's body shifted as much as four inches through changing his thought—and without moving a single muscle! This professor literally demonstrated that *thoughts are things, and their negative or positive power can actually be weighed and measured!*

Where Your Mind Power Centers Are Located and What They Accomplish!

1. The Mind Power of FAITH is located in the center brain at the pineal gland and controls energy, substance, essence. *Substance is the spiritual essence, the living energy, out of which all things are made.*
2. The Mind Power of IMAGINATION is located between the eyes, in the area near the Occipital Lobes. This Mind Power is formative, shaping, and picturing. IMAGINATION is often called the "scissors of the mind."
3. The Mind Power of WILL is located in the forehead in the center of the fore brain. WILL is the executive faculty, the determining faculty, controlling and directing the affairs of your life. *It is your seat of choice.*
4. The Mind Power of UNDERSTANDING is located in the forehead in the fore brain, just above the eyes in the frontal cortex, and controls knowledge, intelligence, and discrernment. It is the idea of all that which is known or may be known. *It is the accumulating and receiving faculty of your mind.*
5. The Mind Power of ZEAL is located at the base of the brain in the back of the neck at the Medulla Oblongata and is the mighty urge, thrust, or impulse that propels you forward.
6. The Mind Power of POWER is located at the root of the tongue in the throat near the thyroid gland. Your POWER faculty is the doorway between the formless and the formed. It is a transformer and directs your potential, ability, capability, and capacity.
7. The Mind Power of LOVE is located in the heart/chest area, back of the heart near the thymus gland. Love is the great magnetic power which unites all the faculties and brings them into expression. Love is radial energy which gathers and binds.

   Love as Healing represents *whole expression.*
   Love as Harmony represents *balanced expression.*
   Love as Hate represents *misdirected expression.*
   Love as Adoration represents *total expression.*

ed of what you

8. The Mind Power of JUDGMENT (sometimes called WISDOM) is located at the pit of your stomach in the solar plexus area near the pancreas gland. JUDGMENT controls your ability to weigh and measure life's situations, values, and standards. JUDGMENT discerns the truth about a situation and balances the faculties.
9. The Mind Power of ORDER is located at a large nerve center just behind the navel in the abdominal region which was known in ancient times as the "Lyden gland." The ORDER faculty represents the idea of sequential action. It controls the ideas of law, logic, adjustment, right relationship, and sequence.
10. The Mind Power of STRENGTH is located between the adrenal glands and the loins at the small of the back. STRENGTH controls the force or power to do, the ability to accomplish. STRENGTH represents the ideas of quantity, intensity, endurance, and stability.
11. The Mind Power of ELIMINATION is located in the organs of elimination in the lower back. ELIMINATION controls the ideas of letting go, casting off that which is undesired and unecessary, and the changing of one's mind. ELIMINATION represents dissolving, renouncing, and cleansing. Your ELIMINATION faculty also controls your ability to give and forgive.
12. The Mind Power of LIFE is located in the generative organs and controls activity, movement, and creativity. LIFE is the acting principle, while substance is the thing acted upon.

Location of
The Twelve Macro-Healing Power Centers
Within the Gland and Nerve Centers of Your Body

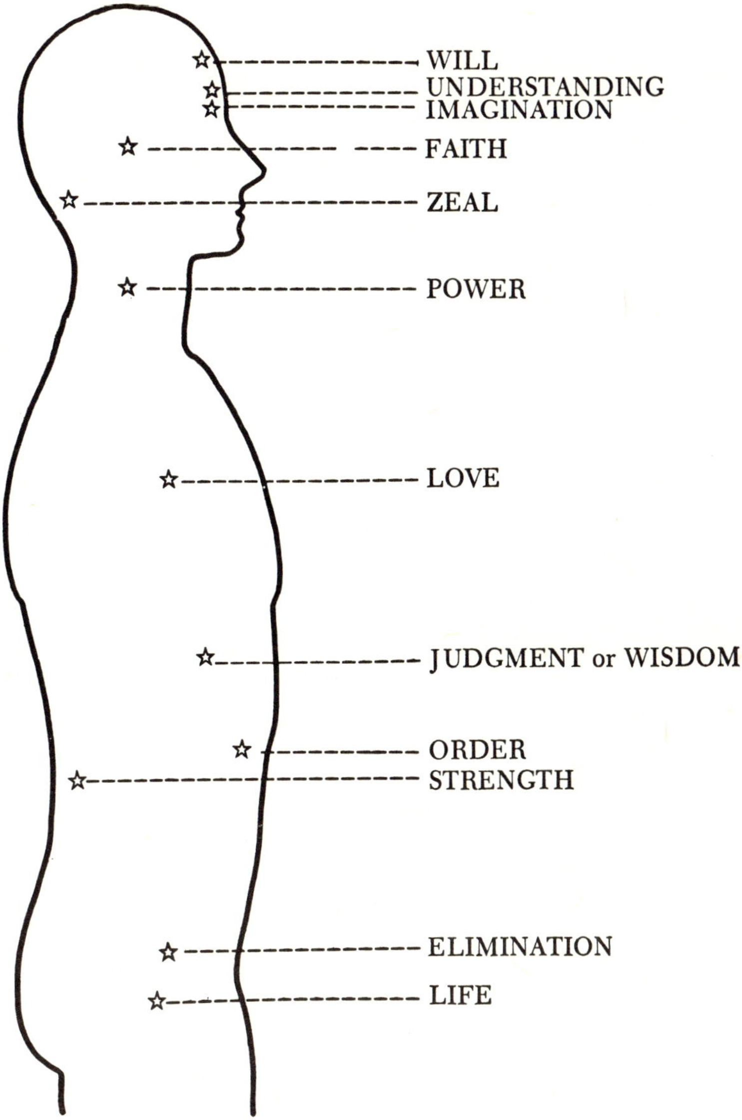

An Introduction to the Renovating Power of the Macro-Laser Light

The almost unbelievable power of the laser beam is an important tool in modern life. Forms of this special kind of light are being used to perform delicate eye operations, to drill holes in diamonds, to cut or weld metals, and even to produce three dimensional pictures. And its tremendous potential has barely been tapped! Because the laser beam is "coherent," that is, because all the waves are in phase and working together, *a laser beam is a force infinitely more powerful and effective than ordinary light.*

Similarly, the Living Light of Macrocosmic Mind is infinitely more effective in your life than almost any other metaphysical treatment. *You can contact this light, learn how to USE IT to transform your life into a magnificent panorama of success, unfoldment, health, and happiness.* Like the laser beam, the Living Light will work for anyone who uses it according to universal law.

I'm certain you have heard of the legend of the "pot of gold at the end of the rainbow." What an understatement! The amazing secrets of life itself are wrapped up in the light of that glorious rainbow, whether it be produced in nature, or by passing sunlight through a prism in a laboratory!

Basic Exercise for Attunement With Macro-Laser Light

It is important to understand that new students will have widely different experiences when they begin exercising for attunement with the Macro-Laser Light. Some will experience tiny flashing lights like small twinkling stars. For a few, the entire room will seem to be filled with brilliance. For most, the light will appear only on the little television screen inside your head. You may experience a gentle sensation of warmth, or you may experience nothing that seems to make sense to you at all. BUT TIME AND PRACTICE WILL BRING THE FULL POWER OF THE LIVING LIGHT INTO FULL FORCE FOR YOU.

Don't become discouraged or embarassed if you seem to be a slow starter. After all, you've spent most of your life ignoring or blotting out this wonderful light, so now be a bit patient while you woo it back into manifestation!

Let's work with the exercise.

1. Sit comfortably, but reasonably straight, in your special chair.
2. Visualize a powerful searchlight, or a radiant shaft of sunlight, shining straight down on you from a point on the ceiling. Feel the friendly warmth of the Light as it bathes you with the wonderfully balanced energy of pure white sunlight. Bask in the Light and feel it washing away all traces of negativity that may be hiding in your mind. Feel it cleansing every cell of your body and every section of your aura.
3. When you feel thoroughly cleansed and centered in the Light, direct the shaft of Light to focus at the base of your spine. Concentrate the Light and all your attention at that point and feel the heat being generated as the sharply focused Light stimulates your LIFE power center and tremendously amplifies the clear, bright light shining there.
4. When the power becomes strong, it's time to lift your focused Macro-Laser Light to the next center and amplify the light in that area. Then, take each Mind Power center area in turn, amplifying the white light.
5. Remain relaxed as you perform this exercise. Take as much time for each Mind Power center as seems to be necessary to built it up to "full power."

How Myrtle F. Used the Macro-Laser Light to Heal Herself of Tuberculosis

Myrtle F., mother of three boys and wife of a Kansas City Realtor, learned that she had tuberculosis, which, at that time, was considered an incurable disease. Her doctor advised her that she had six months to live!

Myrtle was despondent. However, one warm spring evening, she and her husband attended a metaphysical lecture. During the lecture the speaker said, "You are a child of God; therefore, *you do not inherit sickness.*" This dynamic idea electrified Myrtle because she had been led to believe she had probably inherited her supposedly incurable tuberculosis. Myrtle couldn't get the words, "*You do not inherit sickness,*" out of her mind. She began to work with the idea that she could be healed.

Here is her personal story in her own words.

"*Ah! intelligence as well as life is needed to make a body . . . Life has to be guided by intelligence in making all forms. The same law works in my own body. Life is simply a form of energy, and has to be guided and directed in man's body by his intelligence. How do we communicate intelligence? By thinking and talking, of course. Then it flashed upon me that I might talk to the life in every part of my body and have it do just what I wanted . . . I went to all the life centers in my body and spoke words of Truth to them—words of strength and power. I asked their forgiveness for the foolish, ignorant course that I had pursued in the past, when I had condemned them and called them weak, inefficient, and diseased. I did not become discouraged at their being slow to wake up, but kept right on, both silently and aloud, declaring the words of Truth, until the organs responded. And neither did I forget to tell them that they were free, unlimited Spirit. I told them that they were no longer in bondage to the carnal mind; that they were not corruptible flesh, but centers of life and energy omnipresent.*"

Myrtle F. utilized the idea of channeling the mighty power of her thought energy like a scintillating beam of light to every cell of her body.

Healing Power You Can Use Today

REALIZE THAT LIFE—HEALING LIFE—IS POSSIBLE FOR ALL WHO TRULY DESIRE WHOLENESS.

Esoteric principles can succeed for anyone, regardless of religious background, feelings of insecurity, feelings of inferiority, past failures, age, and guilt feelings. These misguided ideas, and this type of error-thinking has absolutely nothing to do with the healing power. *If you are deep down in a dark well, you can still look upward and see the stars in the heavens!*

In order to become liberated into new happiness, a universal truth must reach your understanding. So, the first few times you hear a truth, it may not penetrate into your subconscious mind.

This is no reason for discouragement, however. Simply prepare the ground with welcoming attitudes, and the blossoms of realization will take root and grow.

Feel no dismay over your occasional reluctance to practice esoteric principles. *Not one human being who ever found the golden gateway to a successful life ever started with full account.* The journey was accomplished *one step at a time,* but it is necessary to take the first step. As you may already know, life sometimes offers high walls of resistance, like doubt and inconsistency. Never mind, just *take control, do what you can, and keep walking!*

How Charles Fillmore Healed Himself Of Tubercular Abscesses

When a boy of ten, Charles Fillmore was first diagnosed as having severe rheumatism, which developed into a serious case of hip disease. He was confined to bed for a year, and during the next twenty-five years, he was seldom free from pain and lived the life of a chronic invalid.

Two large tubercular abscesses developed at the head of the hip bone. Charles managed to move about with crutches and a four-inch cork-and-steel extension on his right leg. His hip bone was out of the socket and stiff. His leg shriveled and ceased to grow. Eventually his entire right side became involved; his right ear was deaf and his right eye weak. From hip to knee, his leg was a glassy adhesion with little sensation.

When Charles F. saw his wife's miraculous healing occur, he could no longer ignore the fact that a great and wonderous power was at work. Charles began applying the same Macro-Laser Light healing treatment as Myrtle had used. For several months the response was slight, but he felt better and began to be able to hear in his right ear. Gradually more feeling returned to his leg. Then, the ossified joint began to get limber, and the shrunken flesh filled out until the right leg was almost equal to the left leg. Next, Charles discarded the cork-and-steel extension and wore an ordinary shoe with a double heel about an inch in height. The right leg became almost as large as the left. Muscles were restored and became active.

Charles was healed and, several years later, wrote extensively about the healing power of Macrocosmic Mind.

Infinite Healing Power And How to Use It

The true method of healing does not lie in some magic ritual, such as wand-waving, visiting shrines, touching relics, wearing talismans, bathing in certain waters, but rather in the *mental response* you have toward the indwelling infinite healing Presence of Macrocosmic Mind.

The Macro-Mind Therapist knows what he is doing, and why he is doing it! He trusts the Laws of Healing . . .

> THE LAW OF MIND ACTION ACTIVATES WHATEVER YOU IMPRESS UPON YOUR SUBCONSCIOUS MIND AND EXPRESSES IN LIKE MANNER AS FORM, FUNCTION, EXPERIENCE, AND EVENTS.

You have an infinite healing tool in the Macro-Laser Light, which can literally dissolve everything unlike itself in your mind, body, and affairs.

Will you begin to recognize the uncomfortable areas in your life with the eyes of esoteric insight, and start now to banish them with the greater light of Truth. Today isn't too early to begin! Invoke the renewing, restoring, power of life and health first by making yourself fully receptive to it, and then by letting it work through you.

Place the healing forces of the Universe on your side through:

- Becoming aware of the tremendous Cosmic forces already within you. Allow them to be awakened, revealed, and put to *practical* use.
- Realizing that joining forces with these powers is the same as joining forces with yourself; for a mind divided against itself cannot be a healthy mind!

There's a New World in the Making!

One minute the mind is so clouded that the meaning of life is entirely obscure. Perhaps this sense of confusion will last many minutes, or even years. During this time—whatever its duration—we long for the "magical click" that turns on security, develops serenity, provides clarity of thought, and returns us to an awareness of our own function in the world. IT ALWAYS COMES! As day follows night, and order is created out of chaos, so the human mind makes countless breakthroughs into new phases of consciousness. *This is the overcoming power of man.*

Yes, friends, there is a glorious new world in the making! It's a world of peace, beauty, and love. It is the manifestation of all man's highest and noblest dreams. *And it is at hand!*

Although evidence and popular opinion may often seem to indicate exactly the opposite, there are many who know this new world, for they have seen it. They have seen it through one of the greatest gifts known to man—VISION! This vision is called by many names: foresightedness, seeing through appearances, faith. Each one of us has this ability. You have this ability, you only need to become aware of it and use it!

MACRO-MIND "HEALING" MOTIVATORS

1. It is time the whole world realized that disease is not so much in the body as it is in the mind: not so much in one's nerves and glands as it is in the mind powers located in these nerves and glands.
2. Health does not come and go. Health is eternally present! Our awareness and attitude toward abundant health is what fluctuates!
3. The might Macrocosmic Current within you carries all the healing power you can ever need or use.
4. The purification of your mind is the first step necessary to permanent healing.
5. You have been using, and/or misusing, your twelve mind powers or faculties since the day you were born. And, you have been reaping a constructive or destructive result.
6. Misuse of any one of your mind powers brings an almost immediate health reaction to some part of your body.
7. Life is a form of energy and has to be guided and directed by your intelligence. Decree Macro-Mind Intelligence by speaking positive, powerful words of truth.
8. Your superconscious activity of mind awakens and activates the most potent form of energy known to man—Macrocosmic Energy.

9. You can begin right now to develop the supra-colossal power of your mind by affirming often whatever good you desire. "All things are possible to him who believes!"
10. Healing is not a new theraputic system and its objectives are not merely physical restoration, but a complete cleansing of the mind, body, and affairs through the Higher Laws of Macrocosmic Mind.
11. Conflict arises when your personal ideas contradict what is universally true!
12. Remember, Universal Substance is unlimited. You can't overuse, but you can misuse—and it is the misuse that causes mankind's problems!

9

How to Release the Intelligent Healing Power of Your Mind

Caruso, the great operatic tenor, once was struck with stage fright. His throat became paralyzed by intense fear which caused muscle constriction. Only moments remained before he had to walk out on the stage and sing—but how could he? Panic crawled into his mind as visions of ridicule from his fans slowly formed.

But Caruso was in control. Suddenly he shouted at the stage hands who surrounded him, "*The Little Me wants to strangle the Big Me within!*" Then he firmly said to the Little Me, "*Get out of here! The Big Me is now ready to sing!*"

The call came. Caruso walked out upon the stage and sang gloriously and majestically, enthralling his audience. What happened? Caruso's "Little Me" was the bundle of fears, doubts, roadblocks, and stumbling stones which seem to dwell in the recesses of every human nature. *Yet, these negatives can only do us the harm we allow them to do!* Caruso's "Big Me" was the constructive Macrocosmic Power of his Superconscious Mind.

As Caruso took control of his life and commanded his subconscious power to speak authoritatively to any self-imposed limitation, *so can you summon your true strength and rise to the summit of your chosen achievement.* You, too, can command, "Be gone! I will have none of you!"

A Macro-Mind Secret to Release Your Good

Question: *Why is the action of forgiveness so vital?*

Answer: *Forgiveness is a process of giving up the false for the true, erasing error concepts from your mind and body. It is through forgiveness that true healing is accomplished. Forgiveness removes the errors of the mind, and bodily harmony results in consonance with divine law.*

A Sure Remedy for Healing Every Ill!

Have you ever heard folks say, "There's no such animal as a sure thing!" Well, *there is!* Here is a marvelous mental treatment that is guaranteed to cure every problem situation that can arise!

> FIND YOURSELF A QUIET PLACE WHERE YOU WILL NOT BE DISTURBED AND SIT FOR THIRTY MINUTES *EVERY NIGHT* AND MENTALLY FORGIVE EVERYONE AGAINST WHOM YOU HAVE FELT ANY FEELINGS OF ANGER OR ANTIPATHY!

I don't promise you the exercise will be easy, but I can promise you that *it will work!* Whatever you experience feelings of prejudice against, whether animal or human, mentally ask forgiveness of it and send it thoughts of sincere love. You can do it! If you have criticized anyone, gossiped about anyone, accused anyone of injustice, recall and withdraw your words by asking that person, in the silence of your heart, to forgive you. If you have had a disagreement with a family member, if you are engaged in contention with anyone, *you have the power to end the separation.* See all people and all things in the truth of their being—as pure Macrocosmic Spirit in embodiment—and project to them your strongest thoughts of love. *You do not have to go to bed any night with the feeling that you have an enemy.*

Strive to control your thoughts and words. My son said recently, "*Let the words from your lips be sweet so they will be tastier when you have to eat them!*" And he has a point! You *can be* loving, patient, and kind *under all circumstances!*

An immutable law lies back of this healing method. It is simple: The Universe is created in Love, and as Love. Macrocosmic Mind is Love, and Love is manifest as life. Thus, if we take any action to intercept or cut off the flow of Love through us to another, we are cutting off the life that flows through all! When we, through our negative thoughts, feelings, and actions, cut the cords of Love that bind us together as men and women, we also sever the arteries and veins through which Universal Life flows. These are the times we find ourselves fragile bundles of strained nerves, shaking and trembling with fear and starving for lack of Universal Love.

Be aware also of self-condemnation. If you have accused yourself of foolish action, ignorance, anxiety, poverty, fear, anger, jealousy, selfishness, or weakness of any kind, *ask forgiveness.* Say often this affirmation:

I now let go of all restricting human limitations. I sacrifice these limitations unto the transforming power of Macrocosmic Mind. I am obedient to the law of my being, and I know that in Reality, I am brave, strong, true, energetic, wise, pure, perfect, courageous, and rich. Divine Love is adjusting my life and its problems. Realizing this, I forgive everyone and everything and abide in peace.

You Can Cure Negative Thinking With Macro-Mind Power

Sometimes a burdensome sense of failure or error seizes our consciousness, and we pray with fervor for forgiveness. At the same time we may be unable to appreciate the condition that is involved in forgiveness. This inability to understand probably is due to the ignorance of the fact that the Greek equivalent of "forgive" is "loosen."

An ancient Hebrew book contains a story of Abraham, who was called God's friend. One evening while Abraham was sitting at his tent door, he noticed a stranger approaching. With his invariable courtesy, he immediately hurried to greet the wanderer, and offered him hospitality as befitting a friend of God. While Sarah, Abraham's wife, superintended the preparation of a special supper, the two men exchanged news.

When supper was served, Abraham proposed to ask the blessing on the food as usual, but the stranger refused to agree. He did not believe in any god, and averred that a blessing was unnecessary, and that he would never consent to perform such an action. The men talked rather heatedly for a few minutes, which resulted in Abraham's requesting the stranger to find other lodging for the night. And so the wanderer disappeared into the darkness.

How could it be possible for a man who rejected God to dwell under the same roof as God's friend?

Later, Abraham retired for the night. No sooner had he fallen asleep than he heard God's voice in the stillness:

"Abraham, my friend, where is that stranger that I sent to you this evening?"

"Lord, he was a bad man. Not only did he obstinately refuse to join me in thanking you for the bountiful food, but he blasphemed your name as well. Since I am your friend, I could not permit these actions, so I sent him away."

God replied, "For nearly fifty years I have striven with that man. I sent him here to learn of you, of your honesty, your faithfulness, your prosperity. And you, Abraham, could you not tolerate him for one night for my sake?"

Abraham awakened with a start. He rose immediately and sent his servants to find the man and bring him again to Abraham's house. That night, the stranger was housed and made comfortable. That was the last time that Abraham turned any person away from his door. He had learned his lesson. Some, through hospitality, entertain angels unaware.

It is not up to us to judge others. When we do, we perpetuate a two-fold wrong . . . not only do we usurp Universal Authority, but we *more tightly bind a person to his faults*.

Would it not be more constructive, for everyone, for us to think the kindly thought and do the kindly deed to the one whom we consider to be in error? So we forgive and are forgiven; we loose faults and failures from our acquaintances, and the Universe looses them from us!

How a Mother Healed Her Critically Ill Daughter Through Imaging The Daughter's Perfect Health

TO VISUALIZE THE PERFECT HEALTH AND ABUNDANT GOOD FOR ANOTHER PERSON IS ONE OF THE EASIEST AND BEST WAYS TO HELP HIM REALIZE HEALTH AND WHOLENESS.

Often we talk to someone and express personal ideas or healing techniques. At times, this works adversely for often the person needing help immediately throws up a mental and emotional barricade. *No one wants to be told what to do by another. Everyone wants to be free, and find his own way, and this is right and good.*

So, instead of trying to impress your unique ideas on someone through the spoken word, you can use the scientific, psychological, and cosmic way of picturing the person whole in mind, body, and affairs. Your vibrant, and happy pictures then reach beyond their emotional pride and intellectual argumentativeness into their subconscious soul nature, which then gladly responds and silently works with you to produce happier results for them.

We are constantly suggesting all sorts of things to one another and obtaining results according to the intensity of the pictures powered by our own imagination.

PICTURE A THING AND BRING IT THROUGH, RATHER THAN TRYING TO FORCE IT THROUGH.

Laura C. had been sick the first seven years of her life with various allergies and her food intake was limited. It seemed that one allergy would leave, and two more would take its place. Laura's mother, despairing of medical help, began searching for the mental laws of healing to aid her daughter and discovered the Imaging Law.

After several severe allergy attacks, she realized she had built up an image of sickness about her daughter, both in her mind and in Laura's. Although she didn't want Laura to be ill, she expected her to be. Immediately upon this realization, Laura's mother began to change her mental pictures and expectations concerning Laura's health.

She pictured Laura as the normal, healthy, happy, little girl she should be. She imagined Laura as active, elated, clear-eyed and rosy-cheeked. She taught Laura to see herself in the same way and the two of them even made a Treasure Map of healthy children, happy and active teenagers, and vital adults and pinned it to the bathroom wall.

She removed all medical items from the medicine chest, and spoke often to Laura of her perfect health. Working together, this mother and daughter established a new habit of health after seven years of continuous illness. Today, Laura is a high school sophomore and a glowing, happy teenager.

How to Create and Use a Macro-Living Body Map

A Macro-Living Body Map is a silhouette, or form, of your physical body, drawn in bright, white lines on the Macro-Magic Mirror of your mind. This is a simple tool which you can create and use to aid you in many ways.

When you draw your Macro-Living Body Map, *it performs as a barometer to show you the areas of your physical body where you need to do some work with the Macro-Laser Light.* And you can work in all areas of your physical body with the Macro-Living Body Map. Simply change the color of the lines of the form from the white light to the color representing the following physical areas:

Blue—nervous system
Red—circulatory system
Orange—muscle and bone structures
Yellow—organs and glandular system
White—composite of all systems

How to Balance, Cleanse, and Recharge Your Macro-Living Body Map

Use bright *purple light energy* to recharge any areas in the MLBM which are dim and flickering. Look for any areas which are unusually bright and use the purple light energy for healing, cleansing, and revitalizing, balancing and equalizing, making your Macro-Living Body Map bright, calm, and serene.

How to Create a Vital Energy Bar Tool To Assist in Specific Healing

You can use the fantastic power of your Imagination Mind Faculty to work miracles in your life. You can create a Vital Energy Bar Tool to funnel vast amounts of energy to a specific area for intensified healing.

Here's how to create your Vital Energy Bar Tool:

1. Visualize a large blank projection screen in your mind.
2. Place in the middle of this screen a small circle of dazzling golden light. Now, see this light stretching out into a long, cylindrical golden tube. Some folks find it helpful to think of a flashlight, a "magic wand," or a fluorescent tube. My personal Vital Energy Bar Tool is a flaming sword of brilliant white energy!
3. Get familiar with your Vital Energy Bar Tool. Practice working with it by mentally picking it up in your hands and

directing it toward some specific part of your body. One woman I know projects a Macro-Living Body Map of herself on the Macro-Magic Mirror of her mind, and then blasts the entire Macro-Living Body Map with the Vital Energy Bar Tool!

4. Now, after aiming the Vital Energy Bar Tool, practice turning it off and on. To do this, mentally hold the Vital Energy Bar Tool in your hand and squeeze the end you are holding. Squeeze once, and visualize the living energy pouring from the other end; squeeze again, and you stop the flow until you're ready to use the Vital Energy Bar Tool again.

Use vibrant, living colors to increase the effectiveness of your Vital Energy Bar Tool.

Use Your Vital Energy Bar Tool to Perceive Distant Events and People

Stretch your VITAL ENERGY BAR TOOL from the center of consciousness in your mind to the distant state or person with whom you wish to attune yourself. Let the MACRO-LASER LIGHT energy flow through your VITAL ENERGY BAR TOOL to bless and heal. You may also use your VITAL ENERGY BAR TOOL to perceive circumstances and events at a distance. The VITAL ENERGY BAR TOOL can be used to send messages to distant minds.

How You Can Establish Divine Order In Your Life

Napoleon Hill and W. Clement Stone are two businessmen who have built the idea of a positive mental attitude into a mighty success method which is helping thousands of people. The crux of their method is simple: *What your mind can conceive; your mind can achieve!* And it all begins with a Positive Mental Attitude.

Each day has 1,440 minutes. Invest *one percent* of that time in a study, thinking, and planning session with a better life as your targeted goal and you will be astounded at how those 14 minutes help you get to know the best side of yourself. You will feel the mighty dynamics at your command.

Here is a secret added attraction gained when your goals are clearcut and fully visualized. *You alert keenly to opportunities which present themselves in your everyday life experience, and you are in a constant position to act NOW!*

A *Positive Mental Attitude* releases everything that is detrimental to your highest good. People suffering from physical ailments in the organs of elimination, or in the abdominal region of their body, are people who need to release and eliminate negative emotions. Perhaps they also need to release some possessive attitudes and relationships.

The Mind Power of ELIMINATION, located at the nerve center in the lower back near the base of the spine, is closely connected with the Mind Power of WILL, located in the area of the top of the forehead. *Your WILL, operating through the forebrain, controls circulation of LIFE in your entire body.*

> THE REMEDY FOR CURING NEGATIVE THINKING IS RELAXATION OF YOUR WILL AND "LETTING GO" OF PURELY PERSONAL OBJECTIVES.

Allow yourself the luxury of seeing the "total picture" of holistic good. Thoughts are digested in a manner similar to food digestion. Without proper digestion and assimilation, your thoughts can result in mental congestion and complete frustration.

Take five minutes each day and go on a "*hunting expedition*"! Realize that whatever negative thoughts "eat away" at your mind also "eat away" at your body! Remove the "Do Not Disturb" sign from your mind and let go of the Rusty Hinge Syndrome. Your mind, like the rusty hinges of an unused door, may scream and screech with resistance if it hasn't been really used for a long time, but. YOU ARE THE CONQUEROR!

Personal X-Ray

During your "hunting expedition," look about the rooms of your mind and yank out such impostors as:

- *"If I get my feet wet, I'll catch cold!"*
- *"I never win a contest. I'm just not lucky!"*
- *"Everytime I spot a parking space, somebody else beats me to it!"*
- *"Who would want me, I'm nobody!"*
- *"I'm really not good in any special area!"*

How to Cleanse Your Mind Thoroughly Of Unwanted Thoughts Through the Miracle Of Macro-Energized Mind Power

1. Choose a place where you are not likely to be disturbed. Become comfortable by reclining or sitting in a chair with a back high enough to support your head.
2. Close your eyes and take a deep breath through your nose. Inhale deeply and slowly and smoothly. Then, gently and slowly, exhale through slightly parted lips. In your mind's eye, watch the breath flow throughout your entire body. *Repeat this breathing technique three times.*
3. Begin to use your Mind Power of IMAGINATION and paint a MACRO-LIVING BODY MAP of yourself. The MLBM is full of dark substance—like mud.
4. Picture this dark substance flowing out of your body through your feet, out of your house, into the gutter, and being washed away permanently.
5. Now, picture sparkling clear water flowing through your body from the top of your head, flushing your body clean. As the water flows through your MACRO-LIVING BODY MAP, it becomes increasingly clear. Your body and mind are completely cleansed. You *feel* light and sparkling. You have given your mind and body temple a good housecleaning. All negative thoughts, like mud, are washed away.
6. Now, wash your MACRO-LIVING BODY MAP with delicious golden light. Relax. Proceed with whatever activities you desire.

Recently a counselee related how the *Positive Command Attitude* literally saved her life. She had undergone a serious operation, after which her doctor informed her that the situation was serious and she had about six months to live. Her husband, however, realized the body's tremendous sensitivity to thought and how her body could respond negatively or positively to the doctor's words. When the woman returned home from the hospital, her husband said, "You heard the doctor's six-month diagnosis. You can accept it and die, or you can reject it and live! But if you want to live, you must do three things. First, stop talking about your operation and health "condition." It is over. Forget it. Let it go! Second, affirm the transmuting power of LIFE every single day. *Expect to live!* Third, *believe* in the healing power of Macrocosmic

Mind. Let your life be a living example of what you believe!" He then suggested a daily affirmation stating:

> **I am filled with beautiful, vibrant life. Divine health is manifesting for me now!**

She began using the Positive words of command along with a *Positive Command Attitude*. When friends or neighbors called, she responded with a happy, positive greeting and refused to talk about her operation. That experience happened ten years ago, and the lady told me she had been the picture of radiant health since that time!

Six Miracle Healing Techniques You Can Use Right Now!

> In the beginning was the Logos, and the Logos was with God and the Logos was God. This was in the Beginning with God. Through it everything was done; and without it not even one thing was done, which has been done.
>
> John 1:1,2,3—Emphatic Diaglott

Note: During this six-day Healing Practice, make your denials in a quiet, indifferent way, and your affirmations with a strong, bold, positive mind.

INVOCATION

(To precede each day's treatment.)

I am now in the presence of pure Macrocosmic Mind, and immersed in the Universal Spirit of life, love, and wisdom. I acknowledge this presence and power, and into its divine wisdom now ease my mortal limitations, and from this pure substance of Love bring into manifestation my world, according to Perfect Law.

MONDAY *(Deny)* I deny the belief that race consciousness can reflect upon me any negative thought or condition. I deny the belief that those with whom I associate can reflect upon me any negative thought or condition.

(Affirm) I affirm the Truth of Macrocosmic Mind. I affirm that I am created in the Divine Image. Therefore, I am pure Being.

TUESDAY *(Deny)* I deny the belief that I have inherited disease, sickness, ignorance, or any mental limitation. I no longer deceive myself with thoughts of weakness. Perish from my world all erroneous beliefs. I am now free from them all.

(Affirm) I vibrate with harmony and wholeness. I am free with the knowledge of all that is good.

WEDNESDAY *(Deny)* Selfishness, envy, malice, jealousy, pride, avarice, arrogance, cruelty, hypocrisy, obstinancy, and revenge are no part of my present understanding, and I deny all such beliefs in the whole human race, in my associates, and in my own mind.

(Affirm) I am at peace with all mankind. I truly and unselfishly love everyone. I now acknowledge the perfect law of justice and equality. I love my neighbor as myself, and I will do unto others as I would have them do to me.

THURSDAY *(Deny)* I deny that I have inherited the consequences of anything less that the radiance of omnipotent Macrocosmic Mind. I am a child of the Universe, not a waif on the streets of earth!

(Affirm) I am brave and bold with the knowledge that I am Spirit, and therefore not subject to any opposing power. Plenty and prosperity are mine by Divine inheritance, and I now, by my steady and persistent word, bring them into manifestation.

FRIDAY *(Deny)* I am no longer foolish or ignorant. I am no longer bound by limited thinking. There is no absence of life, substance, or intelligence anywhere, so there is no absence of life, substance, or intelligence in my life.

(Affirm) I am wise with the wisdom of infinite Macrocosmic Mind, and I have knowledge of all things. I know that I am pure intelligence, and I hereby claim my right to light, life, and liberty in all goodness, wisdom, love, and purity.

SATURDAY

(Deny) I deny that I inherit any belief that in any way limits me in health, virtue, intelligence, or power to accomplish my good. Those with whom I associate can no longer make me feel as a "poor worm of the dust." The race consciousness belief of "nature dominates man" no longer holds me in bondage. I now, in the sight and presence of Macrocosmic Mind, unformulate and dissolve by my all-powerful word, every foolish and ignorant assumption that may impede my march to perfection.

(Affirm) I am unlimited in my power. I am now in harmony with the entire universe, and stronger than any mortal law. I boldly assert my perfect freedom. In this knowledge I am enduring, pure, peaceful, and happy. I am dignified and definite, yet humble. I am at one with vigorous life. Peace like a river flows through my soul and mind.

How the Miraculous Mind Power Of STRENGTH Healed People Crippled by Negative Thinking

As bombs fell in Europe in World War II, men who were crippled and had not walked for years, suddenly fled. The same thing happened during a California earthquake several years ago. A businessman was ill, suffering from a kink in his back, yet when fire blazed in the kitchen of his home and his wife screamed in alarm, he quickly jumped from the bed and rushed to her aid!

Often we think of STRENGTH as a vital essence that flows throughout our body, but it is important to remember that *STRENGTH is also a Mind Power!* The aforementioned people unwittingly tapped this fantastic mind power of STRENGTH, and when faced with an emergency, *it was immediately activated, releasing deeper levels of energy necessary to meet the demands of the moment!*

STRENGTH is not physical violence or mental force. STRENGTH is the ability to keep on keeping on despite negative conditions in your body, mind, or affairs!

It is interesting to note that *between 50 and 75 per cent of the people who seek medical treatment have nothing organically wrong with them. Their lack of physical strength is but an indication of the need for mental, emotional, and spiritual strength.*

Your Ten Miracle Steps for Curing Negative Thinking

Climb the success ladder of *Positive Command Attitude* and be a "hundred percenter" in controlling your life!

100%	I DID IT MY WAY! I AM A SUCCESS!
90%	I CAN'T MISS NOW!
80%	I *KNOW* I'LL MAKE IT!
70%	I *BELIEVE* I CAN!
60%	I *THINK* I CAN!
50%	MAYBE I CAN!
40%	IS THERE A CHANCE?
30%	IF ONLY I COULD!
20%	I'M TIRED!
10%	I'LL NEVER MAKE IT!
0%	OH, HELL, WHY TRY?

Check yourself periodically to determine where you are on the *Positive Command Attitude Success Ladder*.

How to Develop a Sure Cure For Tension

Mental tension exists in the difference between what is actual fact and what you may believe, and insist, is fact! Tension cannot exist in fact itself, for pure fact is nontension. Thus, tension arises when you stretch personal opinion away from Macrocosmic fact of truth. *Tension exists in a rubber band only when it is stretched between two opposing points. Allow the rubber band to collapse, and tension vanishes!*

Life does not present you with hundreds of choices of action and then cruelly withhold awareness of the right choice. Baffling choices arise from faulty thinking only. With the dawn of understanding, you begin to live choicelessly and cheerfully for you then KNOW.

Some folks, when assaulted by a critical shock, fall asleep to its lesson by choosing to blame an outside source. The mistake is in trying to escape the shock, instead of letting it awaken you to cosmic facts about yourself.

Healing is not a new therapeutic system, and its object is not mere physical restoration, but a complete cleansing of your mind, body, and affairs through the higher laws of Macrocosmic Mind.

MACRO-MIND "FREEDOM" MOTIVATORS

1. Possessiveness is one of the worst forms of bondage and causes multitudinous health, financial, and human relations problems. It is often reflected in the organs of elimination as disease. Let go! Release that which is no longer part of your highest good!
2. Any negative thought, word, or action can only take up residence in your consciousness if you send out an invitation!
3. Fully and freely forgive. Loose and let go. Not man's will, but Macrocosmic Will be done in my mind, body, and affairs now!
4. Picture your perfect healing and then bring it through into manifestation, rather than trying to force it through.
5. Your body has natural forces within it that can transform it, if that power is consistently released by you through Macro-Mind thoughts and words.
6. You do not stand alone as an isolated and independent creation, but with all manifested life. You float in, and draw every breath of your existence from a Universal Substance that, to your physical eye, is invisible, but which in reality is the only Light, Life, and Intelligence.
7. You think, and your thoughts take form as environment. All your

bodily conditions, your health, your finances, your intelligence, your energy, your domestic and social relations and, in fact, all things connected with your life are the results of your own, or of the race thought or consciousness.

8. The perfectly pure and undefiled life essence in which you live always takes form according to your consciousness!
9. You have the power of coming into harmony with glorious peace, health, and happiness by holding in thought the attributes that are its inherencies.
10. Don't be discouraged if evidence of your positive words and affirmations does not show quickly. You may have been saying "I'm sick," or "I can't," for years. Therefore, a change of thought is necessary before you can reasonably expect a recovery.
11. These are the days promised in which the bodies of men are to be transformed into imperishable dwelling places of Macrocosmic Being.
12. Use the following miracle-working metaphysical healing affirmation frequently.

I am infinitely more than my physical body. Because I am infinitely more than physical matter, I can perceive that which is greater than the physical world. Therefore, I desire to expand, to experience, to know, to understand, to control, and to use the great Universal Energies and Energy Systems as may be beneficial and constructive to me and in my life.

10

How to Dissolve Evil Forces With Macro-Mind Power

God is my Father. Nature is my Mother. The Universe is my way. Eternity is my kingdom. Immortality is my Life. The Mind is my house. Truth is my worship. Love is my Law. Form is my manifestation. Conscience is my guide. Peace is my shelter. Experience is my school. Obstacle is my lesson. Difficulty is my stimulant. Joy is my hymn. Pain is my warning. Work is my blessing. Light is my realization. Friend is my companion. Adversary is my instructor. Neighbor is my brother. Struggle is my opportunity. Future Time is my promise. Equilibrium is my attitude. Order is my path. Beauty is my ideal. Perfection is my Destiny.

From *Wonder Healers of the Philippines*
Harold Sherman, Author-Lecturer

How to Overcome the Strangling Fear of the Unknown

Somebody said that it couldn't be done,
But he, with a chuckle, replied
That maybe it couldn't, but he would be one
Who wouldn't say "no" 'til he tried.
So he knuckled right in with a trace of a grin
On his face. If he worried he hid it.
He started to sing as he tackled the thing
That couldn't be done, *and he did it!*

Adelaide Kennerly

Whenever you place limits on your ability to think, to plan, to execute, you are limiting yourself to manpower; you are disconnecting yourself mentally from Macrocosmic Power—and it is with Macro-Mind Power that all things are possible.

"Can't" is, perhaps, the greatest of all barriers to accomplishment.

Leaners are leaners because they are not connecting with the tremendous flow of Macro-Mind Power. Leaders are leaders because they are connecting with the most powerful force in the universe—Macro-Mind Power! The "can'ts" and the "cans" are going in opposing directions. The "cans" proceed ever onward and upward, making gigantic strides toward the perfection of themselves and their world. The "can'ts" sink into the oblivion of their own discouragement and suffocate . . . yet the exhibition of a minute amount of FAITH would elevate them to a level above their situation.

This earth, this planet upon which you live, is an expression of Macrocosmic Mind. Heaven is here—right within you—all about you, right this very minute. Heaven isn't a place to be found only after the spirit takes leave of its earthly habitat. There is no surer way to close the blinds of heaven on life, love, enthusiasm, and accomplishment than to acknowledge a "can't" attitude. "I can't," stupifies the mind and nullifies forward propulsion.

Fear Can Be Overcome

Fear is cast out by perfect love. To know perfect Macrocosmic Love is to be selfless, and to be selfless is to be without fear. The Macro-conscious person is filled with quietness and confidence for he is centered in the "I can," *Positive Mental Attitude*. There is no limit to what you can do physically, mentally, materially if you maintain the "I can" spirit. The more good you express, the more of life you live and enjoy, the more good comes to you, and the more you can give to the world.

A Cosmic Look at Fear

Macrocosmic Mind offers you many powerful tools to manipulate material substance and create various objects that are useful to you in your material life. But *without the conscious awareness of the soul and its power and intelligence, it is impossible for you or any human being, with their bodies living in the material world, to use correctly what you have been able to create with the great genius impelled from the soul.* Therefore, mind, having created wonderful and powerful material objects, has become the source of great unhappiness for most people.

> Most people are living in the abject depressive atmosphere of fear. And this fear is the very direct result of our inability to contact the soul. People who are not aware of the positive, creative intelligent wisdom and inspiration of the soul, which is the divine nature—and who, as a matter of fact, would deny the existence of such a thing—are automatically thrown back in their conscious into the other element of their life, which is *matter.* And matter, being of the material world, produces fear, which, in the early stages of the evolution of life was very positive and productive. It was needed to guide the instinctive intelligence of the lower forms of nature into the correct use of themselves and their environment so that they could preserve themselves as long as possible.
>
> This is the reason why we see in the lower forms of life this terrific thing called fear. Fear keeps them from being completely destroyed more rapidly by other forms of life and by the human race, which is so greedy and avaricious that it wants to destroy them. For them, fear plays a positive role.
>
> So spake A. A. Taliaferro.

For us, however, fear, which is in our lower physical consciousness and is a part of the instinctive nature, is the basis for all so-called sin. *It is the source of all the mistakes we make.* One who is riddled by fear invariably finds it impossible to concentrate his mind in order to think. He cannot use even what knowledge he has or what memory he has been able to store up. In a state of fear, which is the tremendous vibration of the emotional nature trying to rid itself of some threat, it is impossible for the mind to concentrate itself and become still so it can attune itself to Macrocosmic Mind.

Macrocosmic Mind Is The Very Opposite of Fear

The divine nature of the soul is the very opposite of anxiety or fear of anything. It is creative, it is positive, and it shows you certain kinds of knowledge and wisdom and power or inspiration without which you sink right back down into the depths of fear.

Fear is a painful emotion, marked by alarm, dread, disquiet, and its corollary is depression. *Fear is one of the most subtle and destructive errors that the carnal mind in man experiences.* Fear is a paralyzer of mental action; it weakens both the mind and the body. Fear throws dust in your eyes and hides the Macrocosmic forces that are always with you. Blessed are those who can deny ignorance and fear and affirm the presence and power of Macrocosmic Mind!

Make a Workable Plan For Eliminating All Your Fears

Any scientist will tell you that the proper definition of any problem is the biggest single step toward its solution. Right now, it is important to face the hard fact that you are something less than the perfect individual you want to be, but you are striving to *become* a radiant expression of the embryonic God in manifestation.

Understanding is always the foundation of progress, and a little old-fashioned introspection is good for what ails you! Let's start preparing a launch pad to blast off from all anxieties, worries and fears.

An excellent blast-off pad is a detailed list of everything that disturbs, worries, or concerns you. Carry a small pocket notebook wherever you go for a while. Promise yourself that you will be especially sensitive to every feeling of worry, anxiety, or fear that tries to sneak up on you, and *jot it down in your notebook.* Be certain to make note of even the seemingly small things which make you feel uncomfortable. And do your recording on the spot! It's too easy to forget if you "wait 'til later." It only takes a moment to *do it now.* Don't be embarrassed at the thought of admitting a few fears. Every man, woman, and child who has walked upon this earth has experienced fear. So, you're not alone!

Personal X-Ray

Let's look at a sample Personal X-Ray of one student who worked to overcome fear.

1. FEAR OF THE UNKNOWN, resulting in
   (a) fear of death
   (b) fear of punishment by God
   (c) fear of impending negative events
   (d) fear of lack of control in my life

2. FEAR OF BODILY HARM, resulting in
   (a) fear of automobile, plane, or other carrier accident
   (b) fear of unnecessary torture
   (c) fear of germs and illness
   (d) strong squeamishness about heights
3. FEAR OF FAILURE, resulting in
   (a) worry about effectiveness on the job
   (b) thinking and acting defensively
   (c) unnecessarily critical of others at work
   (d) hesitancy to undertake new projects
4. FEAR OF BEING UNLOVED, resulting in
   (a) jealousy and possessiveness
   (b) feeling of rejection
   (c) inferiority complex and insecurity
   (d) feelings of not being needed
5. FEAR OF BEING RIDICULED, resulting in
   (a) tendency to be shy and quiet
   (b) hesitancy to express new personal ideas
   (c) fear of speaking before a group of people
   (d) being easily embarrassed
6. SPECIAL PERSONAL FEARS, like:
   (a) fear of being inadequate sexually
   (b) fear of being misunderstood
   (c) fear of being overriden by a specific person
   (d) fear of crawling insects
   (e) fear of being emotionally hurt

Your Secret Formula for Eliminating Fear

Continue to add to your personal list and ten days should be a respectible time to gather a representative sample of your haunting fears. Next, arrange your fears in patterns or groups, as did the student. Now, start examining these fears, one by one. *Ask each one, "O.K., WHO is your mother and father?"* Where did the fear originate? Question each fear in the silence of your own quiet place and then pause and wait to receive an answer. *You will receive an impression or feeling from the deep recesses of your mind.* Write it down, regardless of how seemingly insignificent. WRITE IT DOWN!

Work with your fear list daily to build increasing understanding. Knowledge and experience are great positive antidotes to fear, worry, and anxiety. Combine your efforts with a good strong dose of *Positive Mental Attitude* resulting from awareness of Macrocosmic Mind Power and you can free yourself forever.

The aforementioned student proceeded to construct a strong positive affirmation and began intensive daily treatments to dissolve his crippling fears. His bold assertion was that Macrocosmic Energy was now expressing intensively through his life, affairs, and total being. He used his affirmation at every moment of mental pause during his working day, and became one of the most positive, strong, and fearless men I've ever met! Here's his affirmation:

> **The infinite power of Macrocosmic Mind is concentrated upon my fear of ________________, dissolving it into the nothingness from which it came. From this moment forward, Macro-Mind Power is expressing through me as poise, serenity, and effectiveness. I am afraid of nothing and I can accomplish anything I choose to do!**

How Gilbert T. Learned the Secret Of Having the "Guts" to Handle People

While I was in seminary training, I served as a volunteer minister one Sunday each month at a large federal prison. I recall vividly one man whose predominant thought was obtaining freedom. Gilbert was bitter and cynical. He had placed himself in prison by his actions against society which were contrary to all rules—social and universal. In addition to being behind steel bars, he lived in a more hellish psychological prison of hatred and unbelief.

Gilbert and I became friends—of a sort. He seemed to trust me after several months, and I gave him detailed instructions on how to use the power of Macrocosmic Mind to correct his mental attitude. It took a while, but finally he took the first feeble steps toward holding positive thoughts for those he hated by frequently affirming,

> **Universal Love flows through all people, and I wish success, happiness, and peace for all.**

Gilbert repeated this affirmation many times each day, and began to concentrate upon improving his lot. Within a few months, he started teaching a "positive thinking" class to other inmates. Then, he began to imagine himself returning home to his family. He imagined hearing the voice of his wife saying, "Welcome home, Gilbert!" He imagined the warmth of his children snuggled in his arms. Gilbert put his Mind Power of IMAGINATION to use. After a while, he began to believe he would have an opportunity to go home because he had impregnated his subconscious mind with the belief in freedom for all people.

About a year passed. I had completed my work at the prison, but one day I received a letter from Gilbert. He was going to be parolled and already had a job. Not long after this news, I received a telephone call one morning from Gilbert. He was free, and he wanted to bring his wife and children by my home to say hello!

Every self power admits that you will find many people who are deliberately difficult and the greater your own self power becomes, the more of them you will encounter. However, your own self-assurance increases and you have the ability to see people more realistically and the handling of difficult people becomes routine and simple.

In emphasis of this truth, a dear friend who is a strong self-power reduces the entire procedure to one word—"GUTS!"

This one word is the only key you need. Underscore it heavily and place it prominently in the front of your mind. It means, *have the guts or courage to stand strong in what you believe, and don't be afraid to trample all that is less than good beneath your feet!* Have the courage to ignore that which you wish no part of, and be unconcerned that you might become unpopular with tiny people. *You can rise above all limitations!*

How You Can Use the MACRO-LASER LIGHT As Your Amazing White Light of Protection

Everyone has an aura. Some scientists call this aura, radioactivity, and others call it the human atmosphere. Your personal magnetism has its origin in your aura. The purpose of your protective aura is to protect you from all physical as well as mental harm and accidents. To create an aura of protection, draw a mental picture of yourself encased in a radiant energy balloon—enclosed within a circle of intense white light. Do this exercise whenever you feel the need for extra protection.

Use this amazing white light for yourself and for others. Should you desire to protect friends or loved ones, surround them with the protective aura of the RADIANT ENERGY BALLOON. This can be done at any time, even when the person you wish to protect is sleeping. The protection is generated by the power of your thoughts which permeate the aura, and the aura consists of thought forms which create protection.

Perhaps you've built the most beautiful protective light thoughtform ever, then, a week later, you're wondering who "stabbed" you in the back or stuck a long, sharp pin in your effigy! Check backward and review and analyze your thoughts and actions. Can you see all the little holes you've poked in your protective aura with your own little negative thoughts. *The minute you let one nasty little barb loose toward another person, you've punched one small hole in your protective thoughtform!*

You wouldn't walk down the street taking swings at strangers or shooting people, would you? *Of course not!* Well, harmlessness in your words and thoughts is a virtue requiring practice. This simply means that you don't perpetuate or fertilize negative rumors about your friends, nor do you think harshly of those who aren't your friends! *You don't need these weapons!* Let me add here that it doesn't matter whether or not you speak negatively, if the thought is fermenting within your mind, the *action power* is still there! The instant you fire one barb at another person, you've opened the hole in your protective thoughtform. Imagine what a sieve you make when you lose your temper!

When you've taken the time and effort to build your beautiful protection, live in it; carry it with you constantly. As long as everything coming from you is comfortable and good to your enlightened consciousness, it will indeed be your perfect armor of protection.

Make peace with Buster in spite of the fact that he mailed you a rattlesnake this morning!

Become Invulnerable to Evil And Combat Negative Forces Successfully

Affirm regularly this powerful chant:

The light of Macro-Mind surrounds me.
The love of Macro-Mind enfolds me.
The power of Macro-Mind protects me.
The presence of Macro-Mind watches over me.
Wherever I am, Macro-Mind is,
And all is well!

Repeat the chant nine times while you *feel* the protective power growing into a living entity surrounding you with universal protection. Feel its power, and know that it now has a life of its own, with its sole purpose being to protect and care for YOU.

Believe this truth with all your heart and you will positively be invulnerable against all misfortune. *You will have nothing to fear in the whole world.* A mental attitude and a mental cause reside behind all wars, fires, accidents, and calamities of all kinds. *Man is cause; he is also effect!* When man learns to control the cause, he will also control the effect.

The Law of the Cosmic Boomerang

A woman who possesses a strong, unshakable faith, trusting that an Overshadowing Presence is always watching over her, is kept free from any unpleasant experience that might hurt or injure her in the same manner that oil and water repel each other. Mona's belief in this divine protection is so great that I heard her say once, "On several occasions, people have tried to hurt me or my reputation in some way and have experienced severe physical accidents."

Here's one example. Mona had experienced the activity of a new and extremely responsible job for six months when the old demon Jealousy reared its ugly head. Another woman in the office started slinging sharp barbs at Mona. Of course, Mona knew what was happening—all the others in the group kept her informed! But she calmly and peacefully continued with her work unperturbed. Mona refused to accept the situation as real for her.

A day of explosion came when the adversary fired all barrels of negativity toward Mona. That night, tears filled Mona's eyes, for she was human enough to feel the hurt. Yet, she held her adversary in light and sent showers of love in return for hate. She held on to her faith in divine protection and the Law of Justice and Right Order. Mona also realized the law of the Cosmic Boomerang—as you give forth, so you get back! The next morning, the instigator arrived sheepishly at work—her eyes bandaged from severe burns received the night before from an "accident" with an aerosol can!

How Helen C. Broke An Evil "Spell"

Helen C.'s intense desire to grow brought her into contact with an occult group. When Helen realized the group was dabbling in black magic, she left the group. Suddenly, her world seemed to blow up in her face—she experienced a series of minor accidents around the house; unexpected expenses occurred, creating extra bills; she began to have frightening dreams; bags appeared under her eyes; and she began losing weight. She became distraught and fearful and within three months was reduced to a state of utter despair.

After a soul-searching session with me, she decided the members of the group she had been involved with were directing a psychic attack toward her. Fortunately, Helen realized that *all of life's bumps come to teach us some special lesson, and we are stuck with our problem until we awaken enough to digest its inner meaning.*

Here's what action Helen took:

She retreated to her special quiet place. Helen knew that I was holding a strong protective thoughtform for her and this enabled her to relax somewhat and direct her attention to the problem.

She asked herself, "What are the qualities or attitudes in me that have brought me to this uncomfortable situation? How did I go about attracting this situation?" Helen knew that when she was in difficulty, she had to find the key and *change something within herself in order to accomplish the cure.* So, she asked the question of her Higher Self and then paid attention to the answer! Now was not the time to rationalize or make excuses. Now was the time for *Positive Mental Action!*

For several days, Helen meditated to receive the answer which finally came: "*Because of your intense interest in spiritual growth, you have been seeking in all avenues, and have not exercised the Mind Powers of WISDOM and good JUDGMENT. You have sought the phenomenon ahead of the fundamental truth. You need a change of attitude to realize that the foundation of a house must first be laid before the drapes can be hung!*"

"*It's time for you to adopt a completely positive and patient approach; clean yourself up mentally and psychologically; realize you do not have to accept anything from anyone else—even negative, evil thoughts—and get on with the task of living a beautiful life!*"

Helen understood the lesson of her situation and sent the call for help loud and clear: "*Beloved Macrocosmic Mind, I am doing my best to assimilate my lesson and change for the better. Please help me unfold my growth in avenues that are prosperous and good and protect me from anything less than my highest good!*"

Then she kept the faith! One month later, Helen was again the poised, lovely woman I had seen earlier.

How to "Turn the Tables" on Someone Who Is "Out to Get You!"

You're not the only person who is seeking to build his power, influence, and control over people! The more vast your self-power circle becomes, the more people you will meet who are exercising the same techniques. And whether you wish it or not, and despite your efforts to avoid it, a power duel will often develop with some of these people. When it does, you can't bow out of it, or back away from it.

It is important to allow your own self-power to assert itself—but don't try to wield it as a weapon. Remember, *the only "powers" who will try to assert their superiority are false powers.* Such powers have the inner knowing that they can only *wield* power and *are not the real power* itself! Consequently, they fear true self-power, seeing it as something they must combat (regardless of how unpushing you may be) in order to preserve their own "power" in any area.

Your first key in winning in a power duel is to *never display your superiority!* Merely, let your own self-power assert itself in a natural way and you will be superior. When you deliberately stand-off from the show-of-power game, you immediately stand out as a winner, to both spectators and participants. Although the Stand Off Technique is simply that and nothing more, most people find it difficult because they can't resist the tendency to vie with those who brag or try to display power.

Your second key in winning in a power duel is to *know the Truth that the only reason a power duel ever occurs is because another "power" sees himself at his maximum, and knows he cannot step above or beyond you, and therefore, tries to reduce you to his level.*

This is the only avenue he sees to streak ahead of you. A false power person is like an armless man on a mountain ledge—*he's there only because some agency put him there.* He's unequipped to climb to that level himself and he is therefore envious of all others who can climb. As a result, he does everything possible to keep others from reaching his ledge and going beyond him.

A boss for whom I once worked told me during a time of severe testing of my self-power by office co-workers, "The only thing you can do to escape this pack of hungry dogs is to climb a little higher so they can't snap at your heels." He was right! Maintain your dignity, poise, and belief in yourself and you will be surrounded by a protective shell of armor that all the biting and kicking and barb-tossing and trickery can't penetrate!

MACRO-MIND "PROTECTION" MOTIVATORS

1. **Tackle the thing that "can't be done" and sing to yourself as you do it!**
2. **Make a sample list of your personal fears, then study and understand and eliminate them.**
3. **Fear is overcome by knowledge, familiarity, and by facing it with the awareness that fear has no power over you other than the power you allow it to exert.**

4. Faithfully renew your contact with Macro-Mind Power literally hundreds of times a day if necessary, until you establish the perfect poise and effectiveness you desire.
5. Always remember that the whole secret of dealing with and handling people is in having the "guts" to do so!
6. You are better equipped for success, and have a far greater opportunity to achieve it, than all others who have preceded you.
7. Eradicate fear by joining mentally and emotionally with the Macro-Presence within you.
8. Fear is behind many physical ailments. Fill your mind with love and good will and experience freedom.
9. Fear of failure will attract failure. Expect success, and good fortune will smile upon you.
10. I will stand still in the face of all seeming evil and negativity, and remind myself that the all-powerful Universal Law of Justice and Right Order is beyond man-made laws and Universal Justice prevails.
11. No one can hate and be happy and healthy at the same time.
12. The Light of Macro-Mind surrounds me.
    The Love of Macro-Mind enfolds me.
    The Power of Macro-Mind protects me.
    The Presence of Macro-Mind watches over me.
    Wherever I am, Macro-Mind is, and all is well!

11

How Macro-Mind Power Can Work The Miracle of Magnetic Prayer in Your Life!

The *Law of Mind Action* includes thinking, meditation and *prayer*. Through the activity of mental attitudes and faith, you magnetize the substance of the universe into manifestation in your world.

You Form Your World Yourself!

If you have faith in the wonder-working power of Macrocosmic Mind, you can form a near-perfect world! Your nearest world is your body—the beautiful temple of your Being. A little farther out is the world of your environment.

> COMBINE AN UNDERSTANDING OF THE LAW OF MIND ACTION WITH CONSTRUCTIVE THINKING AND YOU CAN PRODUCE YOUR PERFECT WORLD—*A PERFECT MIND, A PERFECT BODY, A PERFECT ENVIRONMENT!*

You receive either good or evil into your body. You choose your food; you judge your food. You choose your words; you judge your words. Your words may be kind or unkind as they spew forth from your mouth. A great teacher once said, "*Not that which entereth into the mouth defileth the man; but that which proceeds out of the mouth!*"

That which proceeds from your mouth can defile because it comes from your consciousness. Your tongue represents your capacity for expression, your ability to say good things, kind things, true things. The tongue is one of the smallest members of the body, yet we know from personal experience that *it is the most unruly!* With the tongue, you wield the weapons of sharp, cutting thoughts expressed in words. If you are courteous and well-bred, you don't always say what you think, or, if the thought is not good form, you let it slide by. You may not quarrel, but you may think in a quarrelsome manner; and then you wonder why the thoughts you have not expressed affect your body! THOUGHT MUST FIND EXPRESSION AS RESULT—this is universal law! This is Mind Action, set in motion by the divine *something* back of the tongue—*your thoughts!* Mentally you may have expressed hatred, and physically you suffer as a result of the hateful thoughts!

Your tongue expresses joy, praise, thanksgiving. Constructive words build a perfect body; destructive words will do just the opposite!

Establish Reality in Your Consciousness

The eyes are the windows of the soul. Why do some people have poor eyesight? People have a dual consciousness. They see good, and they see evil. Their eyes are not held to the single path of glory in manifestation. Why do people have diseased ears? *The ear is only the outer manifestation of an inner consciousness.* Someone may have diseased ears because he doesn't listen to the universal voice of Macrocosmic Mind, isn't receptive to this voice, or doesn't *obey* this inner voice!

Why do we encounter hard conditions? *Because we harbor hard thoughts!* When we arise in the morning on the "wrong side of the bed," instead of returning and crawling out on the other side, we rush about and allow the attitude of our own mind to direct the events of the day. A nurse looks for symptoms and carefully notes every bad condition of the patient. *This is not the way of the Metaphysician!* The Metaphysician looks toward Macrocosmic Mind and sees only good. And what is the result? The patient responds because good is the *Reality. The symptom isn't Real!* The symptom is only an outer appearance, and when you can identify yourself with Macrocosmic Mind by thinking of the *Reality*, then a God Consciousness comes into manifestation and *you are healed!*

Understanding the Macro-Mind Power of Prayer

> **In the universal power of Macrocosmic Mind, I place my trust. Deliver me from darkness; deliver me from bondage. Help me regain the freedom I had in the beginning of the descent of the fiery flame from the heart of God. Let Light fall upon me and deliver me. In Thy LIGHT, LOVE, TRUTH, and LIFE do I abide forever and ever. Thy name be praised! Father-Mother, LIGHT of all the kingdom of Eternity.**

Prayer Is the Golden Key To Harmony and Happiness!

Yet, there is probably no esoteric practice so generally accepted and so little understood as prayer! I have prayed many kinds of prayer. Wordless prayers of spiritual anguish have poured from my wracked heart, as well as prayers learned by rote. I have cried aloud for help. I have wheeled and bargained and demanded. I have prayed prayers of thanksgiving upon awakening in the morning and prayers of gratitude as I drifted to sleep in the evening. I have joined hands with others to say grace at meals, recited prayers in church, and prayed, "Thank You, God," while watching my children and husband sleep. In times of deepest need, I have prayed; and I have prayed when no need existed other than the joy of my feeling of oneness with Macrocosmic Mind—and this might be the greatest prayer of all. I don't know.

Prayer means something special to me, and I often wonder how folks who do not pray are able to survive life's problems and joys!

> PRAYER IS SURVIVAL POWER! PRAYER IS A SOUL-STRETCHING, AND EVERY ACT OF PRAYER ENLARGES YOUR MENTAL AND SPIRITUAL CAPACITY!

There are as many ways to prayer as there are pathways of evolvement. The way of the fish is not the way of the bird. Often prayer is speaking, yet much of prayer is listening . . . and the speaking you do in prayer (silently or audibly) is important, but *the listening is even more important.* IT IS IN THE LISTENING THAT MACROCOSMIC MIND SPEAKS TO YOU. It is when you have done your work, and then become still, that all the force of Macro-Mind Power acts!

One prayer may ask for things, another prayer may ask for thoughts, and another may ask for nothing at all, but give everything!

Prayer is a journey you make into yourself, a journey you make toward closer attunement with Macrocosmic Mind. We often think of ourselves as islands, but we are truly mainlands. Beyond the Cape of Self lies the Continent of Being. I am the green plant of Universal Life, and I would know Macrocosmic Mind as the leaves of a tree know the blazing sunlight. I would absorb Macrocosmic Mind and, in turn, be absorbed in Cosmos. I would make Macrocosmic Mind my life and substance.

How to Pray for What You Want—and Get It!

To those who have no acquaintance with the Miracle of Magnetic Prayer, the above statement may seem to be a rash claim. Yet, be open and receptive to the idea and give this amazing power a fair opportunity to prove that, beyond a shadow of a doubt, it is more than a mere claim. You need take no one's word for this activity, and *you should not. Simply try it for yourself and see the results!*

The actual working method, like all fundamental truth, is simple. All you have to do is this:

> STOP THINKING ABOUT THE DIFFICULTY, THE PROBLEM, THE SITUATION, WHATEVER IT IS, AND THINK ABOUT THE MIRACLE-WORKING POWER OF MACROCOSMIC MIND.

This is the rule. When you perform this action, the trouble you are experiencing, whatever it is, fades into the nothingness where it belongs. It matters not whether the situation is big or little. Your problem may concern health, finances, a quarrel with a neighbor, relationship problems, love, or anything else conceivable, but whatever it is, simply stop thinking about the problem and giving it loads of your energized thought power. Think instead of the power of Macrocosmic Mind.

Rehearse everything you know about Macrocosmic Mind. WISDOM. LOVE. ENTHUSIASM. PEACE. MAGNETIC MIND ACTION. OMNIPOTENT. OMNIPRESENT. Macro-Mind Power is everywhere, has infinite ability . . . and it doesn't matter how well you understand these inner workings of these ideas. *Sim-*

ply know the truth of their existence and go over them repeatedly in your mind. BUT YOU MUST STOP THINKING OF THE TROUBLE, WHATEVER IT IS. Your activity is to think about Macrocosmic Mind, and if you are thinking about your problem, you are not thinking about Macrocosmic Mind!

Many times I have prayed for things which I did not receive, *yet, never have I prayed in vain!* Perhaps things did not change as I wished them to, but *I changed—always I changed!* Prayer isn't for the purpose of changing things, but for the purpose of changing YOU! Prayer is the marshalling of all your faculties. It is a unifying force. At the center of all things resides a harmonious Will. This Will is Life. This Will is Joy. This Will is Order. This Will is Love. Affirmative prayer produces the activity of harmonizing you with the Central Will of the universe!!

How Immediate Prayer Saved the Hands of Kenneth P.

Not long ago, I was sitting in my office absorbed in work when a distraught neighbor rushed in. Tears streamed down her cheeks as she reached out for my hand and her story spilled out. Her nephew was painting a building while perched atop a metal ladder. The ladder started to fall and hit a high-tension electric wire. The impact of the electrical charge knocked Kenneth to the ground in a comatose condition. Upon arriving at the hospital, Kenneth's family learned he suffered extremely bad burns around his chest, face, and hands. In fact, the doctor feared Kenneth's hands would have to be amputated. Surgery was scheduled for sometime the next day. Kenneth's aunt, who was in my office, was requesting that we place Kenneth's name in our prayer box.

"We will go further than that. We will hold a special time of healing prayer for Kenneth during our regular prayer service tonight," I told her.

Next morning, during the middle of a class, the door again burst open and the neighbor's daughter rushed in, laughing, crying simultaneously.

"Last night he moved his fingers," she cried.

"Wonderful!"

"And this morning, he is able to move his fingers more easily and the doctor said a miracle had happened! Surgery is postponed until the doctor determines whether Kenneth's hands will start to heal. Amputation may not be necessary!"

Well, everyone paused and with joy-filled hearts said, "Praise God!"

About a week later, I learned that Kenneth's hands were in great shape and surgery was unnecessary. Isn't this a great example of the tremendous power contained in prayer!

Cosmic Interpretation of The Lord's Prayer

Perhaps no two persons pray exactly alike. For example, most of us pray the Lord's Prayer—at least we are familiar with it. How many times have you spoken the words of the Lord's Prayer? How well do you understand the words you speak? Do you realize the tremendous *freeing action* it activates in your mind and heart?

The most important thing to remember in praying the Lord's Prayer is to recognize it is a prayer of MASTERY, a prayer of INDIVIDUAL CONSCIOUSNESS, a true prayer of LORDSHIP, and it is an INDIVIDUAL EXPERIENCE.

You may seek out a book, a minister, a study class, to determine if you are praying correctly. If you pray in such a way that you seek the confirmation of others whom you may perceive to be "higher authority," this isn't really wrong. IT'S BETTER TO PRAY THIS WAY THAN NOT AT ALL! But your goal is to achieve the *maximum effectiveness* and the *maximum reward.*

The Cosmic approach to the prayer of the man, Jesus, who became the Christ in embodiment, is an individual adventure . . . a constant movement into the unknown . . . not the *unknowable,* but the *unknown! It is a constant movement into the unexperienced, that which is yet to be expressed through you!*

If you wish to pray this glorious prayer and be properly prepared for it in your soul, in your own mind, in your own consciousness, then set aside all you know. Set aside all present opinions and move to a closer, a deeper, a more meaningful, more powerful relationship with MACROCOSMIC MIND.

Seven Important Aspects Of the Lord's Prayer

We're going to look at the Lord's Prayer from seven aspects:

1. PREPARATION
2. INTEGRITY
3. INDIVIDUALIZATION
4. SUPPLY
5. FREEDOM
6. REAFFIRMATION
7. JOY

Now, remember all you have heard about and know about the statement, "You shall decree a thing, and it will be established unto you."

To simply bubble words accomplishes little. People have said to me, "I must have repeated this prayer a million times and *nothing happened!"*

Oh, yes, something happened!

The wonderful subconscious mind of this person memorized some words! She lived the words, ate them, drank them, slept them, "awakened" them, but what happened was that they were merely memorized words! Of course, it's better to repeat positive and constructive words than negative words, but *you want the full activity of the momentum of power the entire prayer contains!*

Preparing to Pray the Lord's Prayer

Two steps are necessary when preparing yourself to pray the Lord's Prayer.

1. *Consider the action these words describe.*
2. *Participate in that activity!*

These are words of instruction, words of encouragement, words of observation, words of Truth and Life, describing an activity that is *taking place in your own consciousness!*

Isn't it a marvelous thrill to realize that you can never pray the Lord's Prayer the same way twice—*once you become aware of what you are doing*—regardless of how wonderful your last experience was, the next one is going to be even better.

THE LORD'S PRAYER IS AN ACTIVITY, A MOVEMENT, A PROCESS, A CREATIVE ACTION IN YOUR SOUL.

1. PREPARATION
   "*Our Father who art in heaven . . .*"
   You are more than the offspring of human beings. You are the outpicturing, the offspring, of a tremendous Creative Process, the movement of the Creative Spirit. You are heir to all that God is, and to all that is Creative Spirit. *Accept and express this Truth!* The kingdom of heaven within you is a growing, expanding, unfolding state of consciousness and experience. Stop leaning on the *excuse* that you are a frail human! YOU ARE A GLORIOUS GOD IN EMBRYONIC STAGE!

2. INTEGRITY
   "*Hallowed be Thy Name . . .*"
   Holy, complete, Infinite is the nature of Macrocosmic Mind in the kingdom of heaven. Where is that heaven? *It is within the potentiality of your own consciousness!* You are specifically designed to bring into expression the *whole nature of God.* You are to establish direct contact, to experience, in mystical terminology, the "presence" of Macrocosmic Mind . . . which is more than just a presence. IT IS AN ACTIVITY. This activity is whole; it is perfect; it is good beyond anything you can presently conceive. *But it is not complete until expressed!*

3. INDIVIDUALIZATION
   "*Thy kingdom come, thy will be done, in earth as it is in heaven.*"
   This expression takes place through a process called *individualization.* In the scientific field, it is referred to as the "process of differentation." In our language structure, it is referred to as the "process of conjugation." *It is the process by which the one becomes the many; the simple becomes the complex. It is the process through which the potential becomes the expressed!*

THERE CAN BE NO EXPRESSION WITHOUT INDIVIDUALITY.

This individuality, in a physical sense, begins with the

atomic structure of the universe. An atom is nothing but energy with a certain wave pattern and relationship. Acknowledge first your Source—Macrocosmic Mind. You can't go further into probing into it until you start to become it. Next, agree to allow this process to take place within you. Each individual has the potential of the Whole.

Developing consciousness contains three elements:

A. Awareness—become aware of this potential within you.
B. Awareness ripens into understanding—an understanding springing from first-hand experience.
C. Understanding matures into a working knowledge that is practical and can be *applied in your everyday life*.

4. SUPPLY

"*Give us this day our daily bread . . .*"

Now, you start to claim your divine inheritance. First, you surrendered to the idea of wholeness, completeness. Next, you surrendered to the idea of your individual expression of the Creative Source. Now you can claim your birthright! You don't have to live by bread alone—whether it's rye or raisin bread! *You can partake of the whole of the feast!!!* When you enter into Spirit, you will find yourself in an absolutely unlimited realm!!!

Here's an example:

Have you ever run out of Love? Have you ever begun to express even a portion of ALL that is available to you? *Love is absolutely unlimited!* It doesn't make any difference how much love you ask for, accept, and express—it's going to improve you, improve your relationships, improve your world. And there shall always be plenty of Love left over! Yet, Love is only a portion of your daily bread—you can also have Joy, Peace, Happiness, Fulfillment, Abundance in all things. *You can have all the Life you are capable of express ing today!*

Have you ever watched a bird sing? He sings because the universe gave him a song that is too big for him and he can't keep it locked up inside. Sitting on his branch, he just kind of hiccups notes of harmony as the current of energy of the Creative Spirit flows through him.

Now, you certainly don't need hiccups, but there should be this same bubbling up and expression and expansion of livingness flowing through you.

5. FREEDOM

"And forgive us our debts, as we also have forgiven our debtors. And lead us not into temptation, but deliver us from evil."

We need forgiveness, an awakening within ourselves before we can handle this powerful new energy. The word *debt* or *debts* is closely related to the root word of *habit* or *habits*, and means a state or a condition of being. Therefore, we are saying, "forgive us of our old, inferior, and inadequate ways of observing life." In other words, help us get rid of these old habits or limitations.

YOU CAN MANIFEST THE POWER TO RULE YOUR MIND!

You can change your thinking, change your basic beliefs, change all limitations under which you have been operating because they are inadequate to handle this new current of life, and love, and joy. *Set aside your own self-made fabrications and limitations. Be willing to give yourself a chance. Forgive yourself and let go of any idea of failure.* If you really want to be a free person, you're in for a real experience because your entire conscious and subconscious concepts and beliefs and attitudes toward life, your fellowman, Macrocosmic Mind, and yourself are in for a fantastically terrific change!

Sig P. told me his personal experience . . .

"I was a freshman in college who had been brought up in a religious atmosphere that stressed the "hellfire and damnation" approach to Macrocosmic Mind. One Sunday, the minister (a fine man, but somewhat mistaken in his concepts!) gave a real lulu of a sermon regarding what was going to happen to us poor worthless sinners when God finally cornered us in Hell. Something in me rebelled and I blew up and afterwards approached the minister and said, 'Pastor, if you're right, I'd rather do business with the Devil than this God you're yelling about. At least I can trust the Devil—He's a stinker all the time, but I simply can't figure out this God you're talking about!'

"Well, the minister assured me that I had committed the unpardonable sin and was going to spend eternity in a place with extremely hot temperatures. Not only that, but he also proceeded to tell my parents what I'd said and what a state I was in! Of course, others in the church caught wind of my action and concluded that I was obviously headed the wrong way.

"But something in me had rebelled so strongly that there was no turning back. So I said to myself. 'O.K., I'm going to have to tough it through.' This was my conscious reaction. Then I had to clean house with my subconscious. For six months I was absolutely the most miserable and frightened man on the face of the earth. I didn't dare turn a corner before looking into the sky to be sure a cloud wasn't lurking where God waited to hurl a thunderbolt at me to get even with me. It took six months for me to work through this error thinking because the old concept of Macrocosmic Mind had been so deeply ingrained in me."

6. REAFFIRMATION

   "For thine is the kingdom, and the power, and the glory, forever."

   It is impossible for you not to individualize the nature of Macrocosmic Mind, because the nature of Macrocosmic Mind includes your individuality. *The rays are not the sun, the sun becomes the rays!* And incidentally, some of our modern scientists have concluded that the sun isn't hot at all, that the sun is merely a radiator of energy. Here is reaffirmation of the whole process of the Lord's Prayer:

"Thine is the kingdom"— *the nature, the potential*
"Thine is the power"— *the consciousness through which the nature is expressed*
"Thine is the glory"— *The perfect expression of the manifestation.*

THE ONLY WAY YOU CAN GET TO HEAVEN IS TO GROW INTO IT!

True heaven is the potential within you brought into magnificent expression through the raising of your own consciousness. The only health, the only wealth, the only happiness, the only love, the only joy you can ever have is that which can be expressed in and through you!

7. JOY

Let your light shine so the kingdom of heaven may be expressed!

As Emerson pointed out so beautifully and I paraphrase, "What you are makes such a tremendous racket that I simply can't hear what you're saying!"

As you grow an inner joy bubbles up, and inner light shines and radiates through you. A deep and growing sense of gratitude for the privilege of living and giving expression to this marvelous spirit that is you becomes more active.

Personal X-Ray

Can you sincerely pray the Lord's Prayer? Check-point yourself in the following areas:

You cannot say "Our" if you live in a water-tight and exclusive spiritual compartment.

You cannot say "Father" if you don't demonstrate this relationship with Macrocosmic Mind in daily life.

You cannot say "which art in Heaven" if you are so occupied with the material aspects of life that you overlook or neglect the spiritual.

You cannot say "hallowed be Thy name" if you, who is made in the image and likeness of Macrocosmic Mind, are not holy.

You cannot say "Thy kingdom come" if you are not doing all within your power to bring about peace in your own world.

You cannot say "Thy will be done" if you are questioning, resentful, or disobedient to the workings of universal laws.

You cannot say "give us this day our daily bread" if you are wallowing in the misery of dead past experiences, or if you are a spiritual bargain-hunter, or an under-the-counter shopper in life's storehouses.

You cannot say "and forgive us our debts, as we also have forgiven our debtors" if you are haboring a grudge against anyone.

You cannot say "deliver us from evil" if you are not prepared to fight it and all like appearances in your world with the powerful weapons of a Positive Mental Attitude and prayer.

You cannot say "Thine is the Kingdom" if you are afraid of what people may do or your neighbors may think.

You cannot say "Thine is the glory" if you are allowing the selfish human ego to override the transcendental beauty of your Macrocosmic ego.

You cannot say "Forever and ever" if your horizon is bound by the things of time and restricted by narrow thinking.

How You Can Make and Use A Circle of Prayer Chart

The *Circle of Prayer Chart* is another effective tool you may use to guide your steps along the journey of a successful life. The preparation of the chart is simple. Take an 8½ X 11 inch sheet of plain white paper and, with a compass, draw a large circle—large enough for you to write in the different areas. Write in the words as shown in the diagram and then follow the twelve steps to success.

As you prepare your Circle of Prayer Chart, direct all the caring, desire, and feeling you can muster into your chart and penetrate it with the power of Macro-Mind Energy enhanced by your own desires.

Here goes:

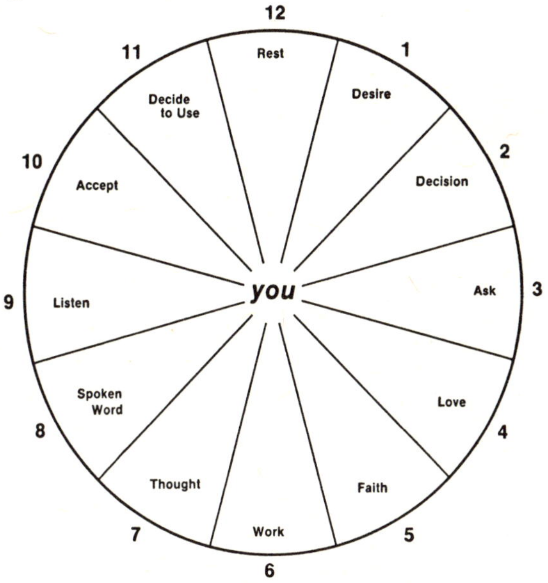

Circle of Prayer Chart

Now, you have made your Circle of Prayer Chart. How do you use it?

1. *Name Your Desire:* Write in this area that which you sincerely desire. All creation starts with *Desire*. The universe wants to help you. If you follow through with your desire, you will receive all the help you need.

2. *Reach a Decision:* Macrocosmic Mind does not force you to accept this marvelous idea of good for which you feel a strong desire. You have the opportunity to use your own free Will and decide, "Yes, I do want this good!"

3. *Ask So You Can Receive:* When you ask in prayer, you place a special order for your good with the creative Spirit and Substance of the Universe.

4. *Utilize the Attracting Law of Love:* The more you love that dream desire you have, the surer you are to attract it into manifestation. *Love is the attracting Law of the universe.*

5. *Maintain Strong Faith:* The Faith you have and can maintain in your dreams builds a strong foundation of Faith in your creative ability and in the power of Macrocosmic Mind.

6. *Work for Your Dream and It Will Work for You:* You can work mentally, physically, and spiritually. Put some action into the picture and direct this action power toward achieving your desire.

7. *Think with Purpose:* Let your mind visualize your dream as having already come true. Think about how you will feel, what you will do, when your demonstration is manifested!!

8. *Utilize the Law of the Spoken Word:* Let the words you speak be in agreement with your desire. Don't desire one thing and speak something else! Refuse to allow words of doubt to come forth.

9. *Listen to What the Universe Is Saying:* Listen to the voice of Macrocosmic Mind speaking to you of all good, unlimited, and yours to claim!

10. *Accept Your Good:* Some folks don't know how to accept their good when it falls into their laps. Be gracious and accept the answer to your prayer when it comes, and also accept the responsibility it brings through your action and words.

11. *Decide to use Your Good:* When your good comes, put it into circulation! *Circulation is another Law of Life—Use it, or Lose*

it! Use what you have to get more of anything you want. Allow your mind to be generous and open.

12. *Rest and Enjoy the Fruits of Your Labors:* You have done the work. Now, let go and let the universe do its thing. Relax. Enjoy. Be appreciative and grateful for each opportunity that comes your way. Think of the greatness of Macrocosmic Mind, of Life, of Love. And, most likely, while you are in the state between 12 and 1, the Creative Source will impregnate you with yet another divine desire. When this happens, you're getting into the flow of life and you're on your way!

How You Can Use Different Types of Prayer Effectively

A typical bit of advice I give to many people who come to me for counseling is simply, "Pray about the situation. And *pray in whatever manner is most meaningful to you!*" I often think of a choice remark from one counselee who was striving to arise from the depths of despair. Looking at me with all the anguish of a tormented soul, she said, "Everything else has failed. I guess it's time to pray!"

I agreed.

She prayed.

Prayer worked!

Creating an Island of Prayer

Often I work with the idea of an "island of prayer" in the midst of a "sea of chaos." Why? Because I believe everyone can lift himself above the chaos. For example, when I enter my office and the telephone is ringing, three people are waiting to see me with "emergency" situations, the secretary is doing five jobs at once, a stack of messages stares at me, and a dozen things to do looms at me from the desk top, where do I begin?

That's when I close the door, settle comfortably in my chair, and mentally tune out everything except Macrocosmic Mind and me! Mentally I build an island of peace, serenity, and accomplishment about me. I become attuned with the presence of Macrocosmic Mind in my thoughts, feelings, and actions. I affirm:

All things cooperate for good for myself and for all with whom I come in contact with this day!

Then, I let go, and trust in Macrocosmic Mind to guide me into the areas whose need is most pressing, and everybody benefits!

Growing Seeds Need Water

You talk to Macrocosmic Mind—that is prayer. You then become still and listen to receive the inspiration—that is a form of meditation. In this kind of meditation, you desire to become aware of your true spiritual nature, or the Macrocosmic Presence within you. Through this Divine Universal Spark of your being, you can center your thoughts on things divine—the divine ideal, the ultimate expression of good.

Open your consciousness to the inflow of good and then *give out* to others the blessings you receive. As you meditate on the consciousness of Macrocosmic Mind within you and without, you truly enter the great Silence of communion and become recharged with divine substance and ideas of the Universe. Just as growing seeds need water, so too, does your precious growing soul need the waters of Universal Life.

Mediocre ideas can lie dormant in your mind and fail to produce the desired good in your life. *Open your consciousness; draw ideas from the Source; and express what you have received.*

How to Become a New Person Through Meditation

Whenever you desire to accomplish something in life—regardless of what—it is first necessary to have an awareness of that thing and then focus your attention upon it. Meditation is a process by which you can bring your diffused thoughts into one center focal point. It is a convergence of thought. It is the finding that center within you where peace reigns and abundant energy resides. Meditation is a cleansing of your mind rather than a harnessing of it. It is the experiencing of the connection of soul, mind, and body.

Through meditation, you can directly experience your personal relationship with Cosmos and come to know that there is truly no separation from it ever. Meditation builds inner strength. Strength builds security, and security builds relaxation! Isn't the process beautiful!

There are two basic approaches to meditation—Directive, and Non-Directive.

The Directive Approach involves the use of an object, such as gazing at a candle, a rose, a star; or chanting mantras in which a phrase or word is repeated; or using symbols such as the circle, the triangle, a visualized light where the meditator gradually connects himself with this symbol and feels a oneness with the symbol and what it represents.

The Non-Directive Approach is one in which the meditator lets himself be guided by his own deeper nature, letting his personal inner promptings shape his inner experience rather than structuring it with a symbol. You observe your thoughts and allow them to come and go.

There are many ways to sit, stand, dance, and so on in meditation. There are silent meditations, singing meditations, chanting meditations, and more. All of these meditations are right and only you can know which method is the best for you. How can you tell? Simply by *observing which method brings you* the most results. It is the idea of "by their fruits you shall know" all over again!

An Easy Method for Entering The Meditative State

Sit comfortably in your chair or on the floor in the lotus position, or with your legs simply crossed in front of you. Your back may be supported by a wall. Close your eyes and take several deep breaths, inhaling and exhaling slowly.

Now, please visualize the sun. See the light of the sun beaming all around you and feel its warmth snuggling you like a soft, warm blanket. Release all thoughts and cares into this loving Light of the sun to be transmuted into radiant Light energy.

Now, welcome the sun into your heart until you can visualize a scintillating Light right in the center area near your heart, radiating in all directions, illuminating all the dark corners of your being.

Allow this Light to blaze into all parts of your body so that every nerve and bone and tissue and atom will receive its rejuvenating energy. Relax in this state of consciousness for the length of time that is comfortable for you. Then, slowly direct your mind to again become conscious of your physical surroundings and return gradually to a physical awareness state.

MACRO-MIND "PRAYER" MOTIVATORS

1. The enlightened mind is free from making distressing decisions. Use the power of positive prayer as your guide, and you will now know what to do.
2. Don't permit negative emotions to bluff you. You do not have to submit to them!
3. From the depths of your soul rings the truth that you can be free of an unhappy life. This is the call that every man and woman can heed and follow.
4. The good things of life want you just as much as you want them. Open your mind to prosperity. Become receptive. Let them come to you!
5. Clear your mind of rambling intruders, but hold dominant the thought of what you want. Use your creative visualization in an attitude of prayer to bring your primary objective into manifestation.
6. Remember, nothing can get you down for you have abundant power to lift and keep yourself up!
7. A skyline streak of crimson heralds the dawn and a lingering star fades slowly. A breath of breeze pays an early morning call, and birds begin to twitter sleepily. A new day is born. Use it!
8. Prayer is survival power—use it often!
9. Every act of prayer enlarges your spiritual and mental capacity.
10. Recognize the Lord's Prayer as a prayer of mastery, a prayer of individual consciousness, a prayer of leadership, and a fantastic individual experience!
11. True Heaven is the potential within you brought forth into magnificent expression through the raising of your own consciousness.
12. Sing and rejoice . . . don't hiccup through life!

12

How Macro-Mind Power Can Help You Establish a Lifetime Success Pattern

People are becoming aware of you and noticing you as a definite and distinctive individual. Through the efforts you have exerted, you have made those around you conscious of the physical you that they see. And then, through your words and actions, you have indicated that your mental self as well as your physical self is also distinctively individual.

The greater your *Real Personal Power* becomes, the more you and it are subjected to scrutiny from those you meet. You have perhaps come in contact with this scrutiny already, and you will be reminded of it again! So, be aware of this fact and heed what it says to you. *You are becoming the kind of person people sit up and take notice of!* Each increase of your *Real Personal Power* means added eyes and ears are noticing what you do—and as is true with human nature—talking about it and you! Techniques and exercises have been given you to get you on your way to greater *Real Personal Power* and initiate your control. *Now is the time to let your actions and your mind speak for you.* Now is the time for people to see you as a genuine individual Self, an archetype, and not a copy of someone else or a mere imitator of someone else's thinking and actions. BE CONFIDENT WITHIN YOURSELF. *You are to be a source,* not an interpreter or amplifier of what some other human source offers.

Use Your Twin Powers for Success Achievement

I ask you again, what are you currently doing about the dreams you want to accomplish and experience during the forthcoming week, or next month, within the year, or the next five years? If you are simply taking life each day as it comes without exerting too much effort, then you're pouring large portions of your potential success down the drain marked "failure"! And, I'll bet you're leading a mediocre life!

YOU HAVE THE POWER TO PLAN YOUR WAY TO SUCCESS

It is unnecessary for you to simply wallow around in the tide of daily events. *You can live on the surface of life!* Yes, you'll expose yourself to some of the frustrations, disappointments, delays, and perhaps disharmonies that seem to follow close on the heels of surface thinking and surface living, but then, you'll get "on course" and become the one in control.

You have two fantastic *twin powers* for success already within your possession—*your physical powers and your mental powers.* When you use *both* for planning your way to success, the results are happy and harmonious. I have known of people who leaned upon the power of thought and paid little attention to their body. In their zeal to become mental giants, they denied their body its rightful functions. As a result, instead of becoming mental giants, they became nervous wrecks with body and mind both being affected. By the same token, if you try to handle challenges from the physical level alone, you've got problems! Bless your body! Praise it! Appreciate it! Give thanks for it! Bless your mind! Praise it! Appreciate it! Give thanks for it! Then affirm to yourself:

> **I realize that all things come by choice. I now choose to be perfectly healthy and balanced in body, mind and soul. As a result, all my affairs are in balanced order physically, mentally, and spiritually.**

Macro-Mind Power— Your Personal Miracle-Maker!

On a clear evening in the country, or atop a mountain, as you thoughtfully gaze at the magnificent shining lamps of the Universe scattered like seeds of Light in the vast garden of space, ponder the immense areas of Cosmos that are seemingly vacant and devoid of life. Yet, stretching into distances so vast that your mind staggers to comprehend, stretching even beyond the elastic bands of your imagination, is the endless area which men call "space."

This marvelous Universe is an immortal tapestry upon which the Creator, Macrocosmic Mind, has woven bright stars and galaxies, great suns and enormous solar systems. The Universe is the shuttle of cosmic magnetism, whose invisible ribbons of radiant energy connect all of the multifaceted parts of Life into one harmonious whole. Across this "great silence" rich harmonies echo the *Music of the Spheres*, each planet and every star vibrating its cosmic tone down through the spiraling highways of the eternal cycles.

Over these cosmic throughways—uncluttered by commercial signs or human refuse—great Cosmic emmissaries of Light, magnificent Angel Beings, Masters, and Messengers of Truth travel with Macro-speed, spanning eternity, joyously carrying out their missions to help mankind—to help YOU.

Dear One, you, too, are fearfully and wonderfully made. From its tremendous heart center, Life pulses a constant flow of energy which descends from the Macrocosm to sustain the consciousness, health, and harmony of your physical form. While the components have a molecular structure that is fundamental to all creation, their unique organization and function is one of the greatest wonders of Life. Draped over the musculoskeletal frame is the protective sheath of skin; within the body are miles of veins, arteries, and nerves, huge switchboards focused in the spine and brain and other vital centers, a digestive system more involved than the most complex chemical laboratory, and many other marvels, including the intelligence that keeps all this in perfect operation during your waking and sleeping.

Both your body—the body of man and the body of the great universe—are filled with vast areas of physical space, wide open space, in a relative sense. Both are composed of shining orbs whirling in rapid motion. Planets, suns, and galaxies form the universe. Electrons, atoms, and molecules comprise the physical body. Great Cosmic Rays serve throughout the physical universe as ribbons of connecting, energizing beams of pure intelligence, which guide, renew, and integrate the many parts into a single whole. Magnetic emanations from the nucleus and the electrons of the atom focus the subtle integrating power that holds the physical body together in one cohesive, working, living unit. The body of man, this vastness of finitude, we shall reverently call the "microcosm."

What Happens When You Start Working With the Divine Idea of Macrocosm and Microcosm

You gain . . .

- a new sense of inner worth.
- a new, wholesome self-respect.
- the ability to successfully overcome problems.
- the ability to successfully handle people.
- the awareness to stop causing problems for yourself.
- the ability to improve your personality.
- a whole new self-image of yourself as a child of Macrocosmic Mind.
- whatever you want according to your heart's sincere desire and your highest good.
- a stabilizing of your emotions.
- an overcoming of mental hang-ups.
- greater financial propserity in your life and affairs.
- the power to overcome fear, stress, anxiety, depression.
- a greater understanding of yourself and other people.
- ideas! ideas! ideas!
- a terrific understanding of your relationship with man, mind, and the universe!

How Rachel J. Exchanged Her Sorrow for Happiness

What do you do when you purchase an item in a department store and upon arriving home, find that it is unsuitable for you? You simply take the item back to the store and exchange it for something that is more suitable. How about unhappiness? Sadness? Can you exchange these "items" for joy? Absolutely! Let me share with you the story of how Rachel J. did just that!

One evening, while attending a dinner party in the home of good friends, a woman sat on my left who looked miserable and unhappy. I didn't know her personally, but had heard of her considerable wealth. During dinner Rachel and I became acquainted and I learned she had lost her husband about a year ago and seemed to be unable to snap out of her sorrowful mood.

After dinner, folks were scattered throughout the house in conversational groups and I found myself alone with Rachel.

"Let's go for a walk in the garden," I suggested.

She accepted my invitation.

As we walked together along the paths wandering among the roses in the Rose Garden, Rachel opened her heart and a year's supply of pent-up tears and heartache spilled forth. She was so lonely and missed strongly the close and loving relationship she had shared with her husband. Since my first husband had been killed in an automobile accident years before, I could understand her feelings. I said to her,

"It's only natural for us to experience a deep emotional shock when someone we love passes on. At such a time it is the better part of wisdom to release our emotional tension by letting the tears flow. However, it is not wisdom or understanding to continue feeling sorry for one's self day in and day out. This attitude can be very harmful. After an experience such as yours, the time does come when it is necessary to release the situation and let it be resolved through day-to-day living. Why don't you release your husband into God's care and keeping now, as I did mine, and start really living again!"

When we returned to the party inside the house, I wrote an affirmation for her to use. I gave her the paper with the affirmation and suggested that she memorize the words and repeat them to herself 50 times a day for the next 30 days. Here are the thoughts I shared with Rachel:

> **I now release my husband into the care and keeping of Macrocosmic Mind. I promise myself I will pull myself together and start right now to look on the bright side of life. I promise myself to live a new, happy life. I shall become a channel of giving of my efforts and energies to the happiness of others, knowing that as I try to help others, I shall be bringing greater joy and happiness to myself.**

Three months later I met Rachel again in a shopping center and the change I saw in her was simply miraculous. She looked like an entirely new woman. Her eyes sparkled and her lips curved in a gentle smile. She was lighthearted and gay. Her happiness bubbled over as she caught my arm and said, "I must share with you that I have been elected president of my club. Right now, I have so much to do that I simply don't have time to give a thought to worry or sadness! Thank you for reminding me of the miracle-working power of Macrocosmic Mind!"

It's easy to understand how you can become emotionally attached to whatever it is you admire and adore. Both joy and sorrow are emotions. When you like someone or something very much, a strong impression is made upon your subconscious mind. Thus you become emotionally attached. However, when the object you admire is for some reason taken away, the emotional tie which held you and the object of your affection together is severed. And that hurts because you begin to develop a sense of loss. It is this sense of loss that you impress upon your subconscious mind's feeling power, and as a result, you experience feelings of sorrow. Can you see that *it is how you use the creative power of your mind,* and the *way you react to things and events* that cause you to feel joyful or sad? It is so important that you strive to make a determined effort to rise above sorrow and create for yourself that joyous feeling that makes life a grand and glorious experience.

Think Success, Believe Success, Live Success!

Each time an opportunity comes your way which will allow you to express your talent, welcome that opportunity with open arms! You have been practicing the Laws of Macro-Mind Power for the purpose of attracting opportunities to you. When they come, open your eyes and be on your way!

Once you make up your mind to become a shining star in your world, it is necessary that you begin thinking and acting like a star! It is important to *think* you are a terrific person and *believe you are great!* Imagine what it would feel like to be great and assume that attitude. When you do this, your every action will tell people that you are a man or woman of exceptional talent and ability. Go forward to meet life with self-confidence and self-assurance. Do what you are doing so well that people will be amazed at how brilliant you are. And, keep everlastingly at what you are doing and what you are doing will result in phenomenal success.

Since no good thing is going to be attracted to you until you put what you know and believe into action, it is important to *practice, practice, practice,* every blessed day the methods I have shared with you in this book. Breathe success, live success, attract success with every heartbeat. Let your waking hours be "practice sessions" so the magnetic department of your mind, your subconscious, can "crown" you with health, wealth, happiness, and peace and serenity. Become totally secure in *who* and *what* you are. Begin living a happy life today. Let your sparkling dynamic personality light up whatever room you enter. Let the joy in your heart give great inspiration and good cheer to others. Let your caring and consideration for others be reflected in your thoughts, words, and actions directed to those less fortunate than you. Go to it, my friend! Shine as the "star" you are and were meant to be!

Your Ten Lucky Steps in Achieving Success

1. Turn ever toward a closer working relationship with Macrocosmic Mind.
2. Recognize that growth begins within you. Don't blame "others" or "outside influences" for your personal challenges.
3. "As in Mind, so in manifestation," is the law. You cannot reap what you have not sown or grown within yourself.
4. Refuse to be limited by outer facts, experiences, or circumstances.
5. Build a super-fantastic tomorrow by being aware of today's thoughts, words, and actions!
6. Love yourself, your neighbor, and your universe by seeing the unity of all creation.
7. Look about you. Find beauty, joy, abundance, and life everywhere at all times.
8. Listen to your indwelling Creative Spirit in quietness many times daily and be guided by the loving whisperings of wisdom from your Macro-Mind within.
9. Again look about you. Give of yourself in all ways and be ready and able to receive graciously. In order to have bal-

ance, the *Law of Giving and Receiving* must work in totality.

10. Dwell in the universal house of Macrocosmic Mind forever.

Special Clues for Success

After planning your path to success, there are several definite success attitudes that will help your master plan become a living reality. You may not have a stockpile of tangible assets at the moment, but you have the same intangible assets for success as do all the millionaires of the world!

YOU HAVE THE RICH BLESSING OF MACROCOSMIC MIND, THAT DECREES YOUR PROSPERITY AND SUCCESS, AND YOU HAVE YOUR OWN MASTER PLAN FOR SUCCESS.

If this is all you presently have, this is all you need! *Remember, start where you are.* This is the first clue for success.

Allow yourself to get into an exalted state of mind as you think about your success plan and the exciting adventure awaiting you as you work for its manifestation. Spend some quiet times thinking about the invisible substance of the universe out of which your crowning success can be formed through rich ideas and actions. Here's your second clue:

AFTER YOU HAVE MADE YOUR SUCCESS PLAN, GET INTO THIS EXALTED STATE OF MIND BY EXPECTING TO SUCCEED, AND THINKING ABOUT YOUR FUTURE SUCCESS.

The ancient sages knew well the tremendous power contained in thinking about substance, thereby drawing success and prosperity to them. What is *substance?* Modern day scientists tell us that substance is that which stands under and supports every visible object you can see in the world about you. Substance is everywhere present, pervades all things, and inspires to action. So, your third clue is:

AFFIRM SUBSTANCE INTO MANIFESTATION.

It's a good thing to get into an exalted state of mind, to dwell intently upon substance, and to expect to succeed with your success plan, because often *you may have several challenges to meet!* And it's mighty difficult to meet challenges when you are not in an exalted state of mind. But persistence pays! And this brings us to the fourth clue:

> WHENEVER YOU MEET A DISAPPOINTING EXPERIENCE CONSTRUCTIVELY, YOU ALWAYS MOVE AHEAD TO GREATER GOOD!

Whenever life may seem to be withholding your good from you, this could be the settlement of an old score. Instead of complaining about your "tough lot in life," say to yourself, "I am meeting this disappointing experience positively and constructively and I continue my journey forward to meet my good." Don't waste your time and energy fighting every little thing that doesn't go your way. This kind of attitude can only cause you to lose sight of your goal and to get bogged down in the quicksand of failure.

Clue number five is your answer in this kind of situation. When it seems your success plan is being withheld from you after you have honestly and sincerely worked to achieve it, remind yourself,

> **My good cannot be withheld from me. No person or thing can take or withhold my good from me. Substance is working now and my good comes in Macro-Mind's own wonderful way! I claim my good now!**

A Pictured Dream Come True

A long-time business acquaintance wanted to consummate a tremendous business deal which involved two other business associates. Disagreements and misunderstandings had blocked the terms of the transaction and it had been impossible to close the deal. My friend realized that no amount of argument or persuasion would be the catalyst to bring the other two associates into a harmonious relationship, so he decided to turn to the miracle-working power of Macrocosmic Mind for help. During the day, he would take time out from his activities for quietly thinking of the two men, deliberately picturing them as peaceful, congenial, happy, friendly, and reconciled. A series of surprising events began unfolding after he started holding this mental picture—the two men were brought together and reconciled their differences and the deal was completed with wonderful benefits to all involved.

A Seven Day Macrocosmic Credo for The Unfoldment of Your Divine Plan

1. I BELIEVE that Macrocosmic Mind has a Divine Plan for me. I believe that this wonderful plan is enfolded within my being, even as the giant oak is wrapped in the tiny acorn. I believe that this Macrocosmic Plan is permanent, indestructible and perfect, free from all that is essentially bad. Whatever may come into my life that is not a part of this Divine Plan is but a distortion caused by my failure to harmonize myself with the Plan. When I relax myself completely and flow with Life, my Divine Plan will manifest completely and perfectly through me. I can tell when I am following my Divine Plan by the inner peace that comes to me. This inner peace brings a joyous, creative urge that leads me into activities that unfold the Plan, or it brings a patience and a wonderful stillness that allows others to unfold the Plan to me.
2. I BELIEVE that this remarkable Divine Plan for me is a perfect part of the larger Pattern for the tremendous good of everyone, not something that is separate or apart for me alone. I believe that it has ramifications and interweavings that flow in and through all persons I meet and all the events of Life that come to me. I believe that the best way to place myself in harmony with the Divine Plan is to accept with radiant acquiescence every individual and event that is drawn to me, seeing them as the perfect instruments for the perfect unfoldment of my Perfect Plan. Harmony within brings harmony without.
3. I BELIEVE that Macrocosmic Mind has selected those persons who are to be a part of my Divine Plan, and that through proximity, mutual attraction, or need, they and I are continually finding each other. I pray for an ever-increasing capacity to love and serve them and for greater worthiness to be loved and served by them in return. I believe in sending forth a prayer for drawing to me all those who are to be helped by me, and all those for whom my help is needed in order to express my life together with them.
4. I BELIEVE in asking Macrocosmic Mind for all the good

that is mine to have, knowing that when the time is right, it will be manifested into my world. This awareness enables me to look forward to receiving those things which are mine in order that I may be more giving, according to the Divine Plan. With this attitude, my mind is released from anxiety and uncertainty. Fear, jealousy, and anger are eliminated. I receive abundant faith and courage to do the things that are mine to do. As my mind becomes more attuned to Macrocosmic Mind, I am freed from greed, passion, impure thoughts and actions; but when I look to the outer realm, or seek to see what others may think about me, I cut myself off from my own source of supply and minimize my power to receive.

5. I BELIEVE the storehouse of the gifts of Macrocosmic Mind are many thousands of times greater than I am now capable of imagining or receiving. I therefore pray for the increase of my capacity both to give and to receive for my power for both giving and receiving is great. The gifts of Macrocosmic Mind bring peace, contentment, and joy, and thus anything in which I find a natural harmony and peace and which does not interfere with anyone else's natural expression of life belongs to me; any work for which I feel a natural call, by gift or inclination, is mine to do. When I am attuned to that which is mine by Macrocosmic right, I find no barrier in the universe, hence I accept none!
6. I BELIEVE the Macro-Plan for life is a healthy, happy, abundant, expression for the good of all, and that everything that makes me feel happy will bring happiness to others. When I seem to be hindered from doing the thing I want to do, I believe that one door is closing, only so others may open. I believe that upon every closed door is a sign pointing to a better and larger door just ahead. My disappointments, therefore, become Macrocosmic *divine appointments*. This is the wonderful, expanding way of the universe to help me find the inspiration and the guidance and the power to overcome all obstacles so that I may see the right door.
7. I BELIEVE that the main essential of life is to keep in touch with my divine heritage, to allow the magnificent Presence

of Macrocosmic Mind that is within me find expression through me. I believe that the whole world about me is full of beauty, joy, and power, even as it is filled with the Presence and Power of Macrocosmic Mind. I believe I can share it and enjoy it if I attune myself to my Divine Plan and am inwardly open toward Macrocosmic Mind, and outwardly helpful and loving toward all mankind.

I now ask the Power that dwells within me, who has given me this vision of life, to give me Macrocosmic help in the realization of my Divine Plan, and to help me share it with others that it may be a blessing of peace and happiness to myself and to many.

My Transcendent Healing Treatment for You

Beloved of Macrocosmic Mind—Greeting!

From the depths of Integrity within me, where I can know and see with Infinite ability, I see and know you, O Precious Soul, as whole and free, wise and immortal!

I see you shining, glorious, radiant, splendid, and triumphant.

I see you free, unfettered and unbound, released from all error thoughts, and feelings, and actions.

I see you mighty, forceful, strong, powerful, and divine!

I see your eyes sparkling with celestial light and fire.

I see your ears open, hearing, receiving all the wisdom of the Universe for your special knowledge and use!

I see your lips open and your tongue tipped with celestial truth and instruction to others!

I see you beautiful, pure, translucent as the most delicate pearl!

I see you smiling, happy, intelligent, joyous!

I see you undaunted! Victorious!

I see you deathless, eternal, abiding forever in Cosmos!

I see you as the strong and forceful child of Macrocosmic Mind, and joint heir with me and all others to the Kingdom of Heaven!

I see you alive with the Omnipotence, Omnipresence, and Omniscience of Macrocosmic Mind, and upheld in this Spirit of Truth forever!

As I see you now through eyes of Love, so may all the world see you in all your glory—O Child of Eternal Light.

A Closing Thought

The highest Truth you know is but a half-truth. Think not, my friend, to settle down eternally in any one Truth. Make use of the Truth you now have as you would make use of a tent in which to spend a summer's night. But do not build a house of the present Truth you have, else it become your tomb. When life brings you a faint inkling of the insufficiency of the Truth you presently have, and you catch a mere glimmer of a greater Truth rising on the horizon, weep not. Instead, give thanks to the Universe and recognize the Cosmic call to "Pick up thy bed and walk!"

MACRO-MIND "SUCCESS" MOTIVATORS

1. Be confident within yourself. *You are a source,* not an interpreter or amplifier of what some other human source offers.
2. You have the power, ability, and knowledge to plan your way to success.
3. Use your twin powers for success—physical and mental.
4. Happiness is not freedom from problems, but victory over them!
5. Most people use only one tenth of their total capacity for work and original thought. Harness your full powers and be joyously amazed at the results!
6. Your real dreams are closer than you think. Dare to reach for them!
7. Achieving success demands total effort. Beware of distractions. "Keep your eye single."
8. Use the combined powers of your mind and the spoken word to affirm substance into manifestation.
9. "Divine substance appropriately manifests for me here and now."
10. When you rule your mind, you rule your world!
11. Put your "get-up-and-go" power into action!
12. Think success! Believe success! Be success!

13

Fifty Super-Special Macro-Mind Magnetizers for Daily Use

The Ready Reference Guide has been especially prepared so you may have a source, at your fingertips, of assistance any time during the day or night. Remember, WHEN YOU RULE YOUR MIND, YOUR RULE YOUR WORLD. So make this handy guide your personal friend and companion. *It will never let you down!*

1. ABUNDANCE — "Every day, in every way, I am growing more prosperous, successful, victorious, and happy. I now experience abundance in ever-increasing degrees of good."
2. ACHIEVEMENT — "The desire for achievement is innate within my soul. Every experience in life contains showers of blessings for me and I claim them now."
3. HEALTH — "My body is the beautiful temple for Macrocosmic Mind. I am healthy in body. I am healthy in Mind. I am healthy in Spirit. The rhythm and harmony of the universe flows through my being, uniting me with all things good and healthful."
4. AFFIRMATION — "I use the 'yes' action of my mind to claim my good in whatever areas I desire. I declare the Truth that I am a Child of Macrocosmic Mind and I have the ability to affirm my good."
5. ANXIETY — "I realize that anxiety is a form of fear and a negative mental attitude that keeps my good from manifesting. I

	now affirm that my mind is peaceful and serene and I am free from all anxiety."
6. CONFIDENCE	"I am filled with confidence in myself and in my ability. I am a useful and important person. Today, I think with confidence and I act with confidence."
7. COURAGE	"I am strong, powerful, and courageous. I am brave in heart, strong in mind, and master of all I survey. Nothing has power to harm me."
8. ATTITUDE	"I maintain a strong and powerful attitude toward everything in my life. I greet this day with a new outlook. Old things are passed away, and all things are new for me in the Eternal Now."
9. LIVE	"Today I truly LIVE. I establish inner harmony within my own heart and mind and let this feeling flow forth from me into my outer world and its activities. Each moment is filled with life and love and power."
10. FRIENDSHIP	"This day I will be a friend to myself. I will be a friend to others by acting friendly to everyone I meet, by being kind and considerate. I will express good will and cheer. My friendly attitude will attract friendly people to me."
11. SERENITY	"I am always in control of my own thinking and I take a positive stand. I refuse to think along negative lines. I turn my thoughts away from that which has annoyed or upset me and instead think in positive terms of peace and right outworking. I am calm, composed, and serene."

12. SUSTAINED — "Love enfolds me. Life sustains me. Macrocosmic mind is with me now. I trust this Presence to bless me, to heal me, to be a very present help, no matter what the condition or need."

13. PERSONALITY — "Today I will let a smile light up my face. Today I will laugh and be happy. Today I will BE the magnetic personality I desire to be and express myself in a positive, self-confident manner."

14. LOVE — "Love is the pure essence of Being that binds together the whole human family. It is the healing, harmonizing, 'spiritual glue' of the universe. Today I shall love my work, my life, all people. Love motivates my every action and I am blessed."

15. FORGIVE — "I freely and fully forgive, for the forgiving power of Macrocosmic Mind within me empowers me to love and forgive others."

16. PROSPERITY — "I know my own shall come to me, for the law of giving and receiving is at work in my life. I make room for my prosperity by giving whatever it is I have to give."

17. CHANGE — "I welcome all change as an opportunity to grow in new areas of experience. I know that when one door closes for me, another is already opening and welcoming me to accept my higher good. Today, I shall take advantage of every opportunity brought to me through change."

18. SELF-CONTROL — "I am now free from every belief that might in any way interfere with my perfect expression of health, wealth,

peace, prosperity, and perfect satisfaction in every area of my life."

19. IN TUNE — "I am in tune with Life. I am in tune with the flow of Macrocosmic Mind. Divine Order prevails in my life and affairs."

20. PRAYER — "Prayer enables me to keep my thoughts positive and free from anxiety. I pray for myself and for my loved ones, seeing within us all the fulfillment of our every need."

21. BEGINNING — "I am ready and eager to begin a glorious new life. Today is a new day, the start of a new beginning for me now."

22. FAITH — "I know that if I don't have faith and belief in myself, no one else will. I decide right now to achieve great things. I believe a miracle of untold good is happening to me now."

23. WINNER — "I am a born winner! Progress and achievement are my lot in life. I am meant to grow and express abundance. I am born to win!"

24. CONSIDERATION — "Today I meet life with understanding and compassion in my heart. I maintain an unselfish attitude, a sympathetic spirit. Kindness, consideration, and good will are the rule of my day."

25. HARMONY — "Harmony is my keynote. I see every aspect of my life—work, relationships, home, family, friends—all is harmonious."

26. FEELING — "I have a marvelous feeling that something good is about to happen. This feeling makes me feel terrific. This feeling makes me feel marvelous."

27. THANKS — "I give abundant thanks for all the blessings I have received, am receiving, and shall receive. This mental action on my part acts as a magnet drawing to me increased good fortune."

28. REJOICE — "My heart sings a song of praise and gratitude, and my world is filled with peace and harmony."

29. GROWTH — "I give thanks that some things—like Macrocosmic Mind—never change, and some things never stay the same."

30. DIVINE SELF — "I follow my Divine Self and Divine Plan and express the divine attributes with which I am endowed."

31. IDEAS — "I have an abundance of right ideas. Any time I need an idea that will solve a problem or promote growth, I make the request of my subconscious mind to attract the right idea to me. And it works!!"

32. RELEASE — "I become still. I let go. I let God show me the right way."

33. VITALITY — "I am vibrant and vital, alive forevermore. I am consciously aware that my whole being pulsates with life and vigor."

34. SECURE — "I am a child of the universe, secure in the realization of the MACRO-PRESENCE within me and all around me."

35. JUSTICE — "The law of perfect justice is now established in my life. I am thankful that no one can deal with me unjustly, for I believe in universal perfect justice always active and at work in my life."

36. HERITAGE — "Since Macrocosmic Mind is my Creator, I am endowed with divine strength and perfection. I know my true source of life, health, and prosperity."

37. COMFORT — "I receive comfort from the knowledge that life and love are eternal, forever. I am fully convinced that my soul is indestructible, and that its activities will continue through eternity."

38. GUIDANCE — "I am divinely guided, my life has meaning, purpose, and steady direction. Nothing can pull me off this divinely established course."

39. WINGS — "Today, I take the wings of the morning, and soar!"

40. MIRACLES — "I believe that miracles are happening for me now. All I have to do is to *expect* a marvelous and unusual event to unfold in my life."

41. DOMINION — "I declare my dominion over myself and my life."

42. TOLERANCE — "I criticize no one; I judge no one; I express love to all."

43. DIRECTION — "Today my life takes a new direction. Regardless of where I stood on the road of life yesterday, today a new way stretches before me."

44. RENEWAL — "The quickening, renewing Spirit in me recharges my whole being with life, power, and energy."

45. MONEY — "I believe it is my divine right to have all the money I can use to satisfy my every need. I use the money I receive wisely. Money flows to me in a steady stream today from various sources. I am always supplied with an abundance of money.

46. TALENT	"I will use my full talents today. I will express my ability at every opportunity that comes along. Today, I will use my talents for the benefit of people. I believe I can gain fame and fortune by using my talents successfully."
47. I CAN!	"The 'I Can!' attitude is the attitude I am meant to have. Self-confidence is the quality I am meant to express. Through the power of Macrocosmic Mind within me, 'I CAN!' "
48. JOY	"I start this day with joy in my heart. I will invite this joy to remain throughout the activities of today and try to give some of my joy to others I meet."
49. SUCCESS	"I believe in success. I believe in my success. My subconscious mind already knows I am successful, and is working to attract to me all I need to manifest this success outwardly."
50. VICTORY	"Praise God! I am victorious! I have gained victory over my thoughts, feelings, and actions. I know how to attract all good things to me. I am a new, dynamic, magnetic and gloriously victorious person!"